Cost-Benefit Analysis and Dementia

This book is dedicated to my wife Elizabeth,
our sons Adam and Matthew, and my friends
Ian Scurfield, Paul Periton and Milford Prewitt

Cost-Benefit Analysis and Dementia

New Interventions

Robert J. Brent

Professor of Economics, Fordham University, New York, USA

Cheltenham, UK • Northampton, MA, USA

Published by
Edward Elgar Publishing Limited
The Lypiatts
15 Lansdown Road
Cheltenham
Glos GL50 2JA
UK

Edward Elgar Publishing, Inc.
William Pratt House
9 Dewey Court
Northampton
Massachusetts 01060
USA

Paperback edition 2023

A catalogue record for this book
is available from the British Library

Library of Congress Control Number: 2022932136

This book is available electronically in the **Elgar**online
Economics subject collection
http://dx.doi.org/10.4337/9781839105760

MIX
Paper | Supporting
responsible forestry
FSC
www.fsc.org   FSC® C013604

ISBN 978 1 83910 575 3 (cased)
ISBN 978 1 83910 576 0 (eBook)
ISBN 978 1 0353 1690 8 (paperback)

Printed and bound by CPI Group (UK) Ltd, Croydon, CR0 4YY

Contents

Figures and tables

FIGURE

TABLES

Preface

This book is devoted to understanding dementia, and how one can, and should, intervene with specified interventions to help make many of the symptoms of dementia decline. The medical literature has almost exclusively focused on brain pathology to define dementia. From this perspective, nothing can be done at this time to reduce dementia, as no long-lasting pharmacological medications, or surgeries, have been created that can alter the neurological makeup of the brain. However, if one uses a behavioral definition of dementia, in terms of dementia symptoms related to activities of daily living, then there already exists many effective dementia interventions. Some of these interventions are well known, and some have only recently been evaluated, and are in this sense "new." This book focuses mainly on these new interventions.

Once one accepts the reality of non-medical interventions for reducing dementia symptoms, this opens up the field to a wide range of possible interventions. On the list of new interventions, we include years of education, Medicare eligibility, hearing aids, and vision correction. We can then add as a new intervention the avoidance of living in a nursing home, as residing in a nursing home actually increases dementia symptoms. Furthermore, one needs to recognize that the legal system can be viewed as a domain for dementia interventions. This means that reducing elder abuse, and initiating an international convention for human rights, can also be viewed as interventions that reduce the symptoms of dementia.

The medical literature has also mainly focused on establishing the effectiveness of any dementia intervention. The book follows this lead, by examining the extent to which the reduction in symptoms from any particular intervention can be said to be causally related to the intervention's impact. However, it must be understood that, from a public policy perspective, just because an intervention has been found to be causal and effective, this does not necessarily mean that one should spend money on it. While it may be intuitively obvious that if an intervention has been found to be effective, it must have had benefits, these benefits, which are outcomes measured in monetary terms, need to be estimated to see how large they are. This estimation of benefits needs to take place because it is an economic reality that interventions also involve monetary costs. Only if the monetary benefits are greater than the monetary costs should any effective intervention be worthy of financial support. This is why Cost-Benefit Analysis (CBA) is the public policy cornerstone for the book.

Although the new interventions relate to the USA, and are based on US data, there is every reason to expect that the new interventions evaluated in this book would be as worthwhile, or even more worthwhile, in Low-and-Middle Income Countries (LMICs). This is because dementia is more widespread in these countries. For this reason, every chapter devoted to evaluating a particular dementia intervention has a separate section that discusses the relevance of the US results for LMICs.

There are a number of people that I want to thank for their support and inspiration, without which the book would not have been possible. Although professionally I have always been an economist involved with CBA, my interest in the application of CBA to dementia interventions came about more recently. My thanks primarily go to Patricia Brownell and Susan Somers. Pat educated me about elder abuse, shared her data with me, and introduced me to Susan. From Susan I learned all about the United Nations non-governmental organization committee system, where a concern for the human rights of older adults was an overarching concern. Many instances of human rights violations concerned persons with dementia. I contacted the National Alzheimer's Coordinating Center (NACC) and they released a number of rounds of data for me to analyse. The estimations of the effectiveness of all the new interventions were based on the NACC data set. The NACC staff, Lilah Besser, Nicole Barlow, and Kathryn Gauthreaux, spent many hours responding to all the questions I had about using and interpreting the variables in the data set. I am most grateful for their assistance, and the NACC generally for releasing their data for use by me. Finally, I wish to thank Fordham University for grating me a semester off from teaching in the Spring of 2020 in order that I could devote time to writing this book.

Acknowledgments

The National Association Coordinating Center (NACC) database is funded by NIA/NIH Grant U01 AG016976. NACC data are contributed by the NIA funded ADCs: P30 AG019610 (PI Eric Reiman, MD), P30 AG013846 (PI Neil Kowall, MD), P50 AG008702 (PI Scott Small, MD), P50 AG025688 (PI Allan Levey, MD, PhD), P30 AG010133 (PI Andrew Saykin, PsyD), P50 AG005146 (PI Marilyn Albert, PhD), P50 AG005134 (PI Bradley Hyman, MD, PhD), P50 AG016574 (PI Ronald Petersen, MD, PhD), P50 AG005138 (PI Mary Sano, PhD), P30 AG008051 (PI Steven Ferris, PhD), P30 AG013854 (PI M. Marsel Mesulam, MD), P30 AG008017 (PI Jeffrey Kaye, MD), P30 AG010161 (PI David Bennett, MD), P30 AG010129 (PI Charles DeCarli, MD), P50 AG016573 (PI Frank LaFerla, PhD), P50 AG016570 (PI David Teplow, PhD), P50 AG005131 (PI Douglas Galasko, MD), P50 AG023501 (PI Bruce Miller, MD), P30 AG035982 (PI Russell Swerdlow, MD), P30 AG028383 (PI Linda Van Eldik, PhD), P30 AG010124 (PI John Trojanowski, MD, PhD), P50 AG005133 (PI Oscar Lopez, MD), P50 AG005142 (PI Helena Chui, MD), P30 AG012300 (PI Roger Rosenberg, MD), P50 AG005136 (PI Thomas Montine, MD, PhD), P50 AG033514 (PI Sanjay Asthana, MD, FRCP), P50 AG005681 (PI John Morris, MD) and P50 AGO047270 (PI Stephen Strittmatter, MD, PhD).

Abbreviations

AD	Alzheimer's disease
ADCs	Alzheimer's Disease Centers
ADL	Activities of daily living
ANI	Asymptomatic neurocognitive impairment
APOE	Apolipoprotein E gene
APS	Adult Protective Services
AWV	Annual Wellness Visit
BMI	Body Mass Index
CAI	Compassionate Allowance Initiative
CBA	Cost-Benefit Analysis
CDR	Clinical Dementia Rating scale
CDR-SB	CDR Sum of Boxes
CEA	Cost-Effective Analysis
CLs	Corrective lenses
CMS	Center for Medicare and Medicaid Services
CR	Cognitive rehabilitation
CSI'D'	Community Screening Instrument for dementia
DALY	Disability Adjusted Life Year
DAO	District Attorney's Office
DLB	Dementia with Lewy bodies
DSM-IV	*Diagnostic and Statistical Manual of Mental Disorders*, 4th edition
EAFC	Elder Abuse Forensic Center
ER	Emergency room
GDP	Gross Domestic Product
GDS	Geriatric Depression Scale
HA	Hearing aid

HAD	HIV-associated dementia
HAND	HIV-associated neurocognitive disorders
HL	Hearing loss
ILO	International Labour Organization
LAYS	Learning-Adjusted Years of Schooling
LMIC	Low-and-Middle Income Countries
LY	Life years
MCI	Mild cognitive impairment
MIND	Mediterranean-DASH Intervention diet for Neurodegenerative Delay
MIPA	Madrid International Plan of Action on Ageing
MMSE	Mini-mental state examination
MND	HIV-associated minor neurocognitive disorders
NACC	National Alzheimer's Coordinating Center
NH	Nursing home
PD	Parkinson's disease
QALY	Quality adjusted life year
QoL	Quality of life
RD	Regression discontinuities
SEA	South East Asia
SNF	Skilled nursing facilities
SSA	Sub-Saharan Africa
TAP	Tailored Activity Program
TBI	Traumatic brain injury
UDS	Unified Data Set
UN	United Nations
VC	Vision correction
VI	Vision impairment
VSL	Value of a statistical life
VSLY	Value of a statistical life year
WHO	World Health Organization
WTP	Willingness to Pay

PART I

Introduction

1. Introduction to dementia, Cost-Benefit Analysis, and the new interventions

Dementia is associated with aging. With the aging of the world's population, more and more people will get dementia. As of 2015, 47 million (5 percent of the world's elderly population) have dementia and this is predicted to rise to 75 million in 2030, and 132 million by 2050. Dementia will affect almost everyone, either directly (they will get the disease) or indirectly (because they will have responsibilities as a caregiver for someone with dementia). In 2015, the worldwide dementia costs, in terms of medical care, social care, and informal care, were estimated to be $818 billion. This global cost of care will reach $2 trillion by 2030.[1] In the USA in 2021, there were 6.2 million persons just with the main type of dementia (Alzheimer's disease), and the lifetime cost of care for anyone with dementia is $373,527 in 2020 prices, 70 percent of which was borne by caregivers.[2]

Given the enormous magnitudes of both the numbers with dementia and their associated costs, the relevant question to ask is whether we can do anything worthwhile (find interventions) to mitigate this global problem. The good news is that we can do something today that can begin to help solve this problem, if we can agree on what a solution looks like. Obviously, dementia is a medical condition. However, limiting oneself to just medical solutions is not helpful, especially when, as at this time, they have not progressed very far. What is required is a wider, public policy perspective that expands the solution set to include any form of intervention that reduces dementia and is found to be socially worthwhile. By "social," we refer to society as a whole, which not only includes all those benefiting from a dementia intervention, but also all those incurring the costs.[3] A Cost-Benefit perspective will be used to indicate whether any intervention is socially worthwhile or not.

CHAPTER OUTLINE

This book is devoted to a presentation of new, non-medical, worthwhile dementia interventions, and to explaining all the ingredients that allows them to be classed as "worthwhile." Before we can do this, it is necessary, as we do in this chapter, to set out the fundamentals. This involves: defining exactly what is dementia; identifying what are the types of intervention that have been tested; explaining what is necessary to establish effectiveness; and explaining the role of Cost-Benefit Analysis (CBA) in public policy decision-making related to dementia interventions. As a part of the summary and conclusions to this chapter, we will explain the outline for the rest of the book.

WHAT IS DEMENTIA?

The official diagnostic criteria for dementia are set out in the *Diagnostic and Statistical Manual of Mental Disorders*, 4th edition (which are called the DSM-IV criteria) and this is the benchmark for diagnosing dementia worldwide. Two cognitive deficits must be present for the diagnosis. First, there must be memory impairment (an inability to learn new information or recall previously learned information). And second, one (or more) of the following four cognitive disturbances need to be detected: language disturbance (aphasia); impaired ability to carry out major motor activities despite intact motor function (apraxia); failure to recognize objects despite intact sensory function (agnosia); and disturbance in executive functioning, involving such things as planning or organizing. Each of these two cognitive deficits can be expected to cause significant impairment in "social or occupational functioning." This impairment in functioning must represent a significant decline from a previous level of functioning.[4]

In line with the DSM-IV criteria, we will simply define dementia as existing when a person has been diagnosed with cognitive impairment that interferes with activities of daily living (ADL). The Alzheimer's Association's 2018 Disease and Facts Report – hereafter referred to as "the 2018 Report" – also stresses that what is characteristic of dementia is that it affects "a person's ability to perform everyday activities."[5] From the outset, we wish to emphasize that interfering with ADL is a behavioral definition of dementia. That is, people with dementia do not behave as they used to, and in ways that they would want to, or choose to, behave.[6] Dementia produces symptoms that interfere with behavior. It is for this reason that we will examine throughout the book interventions that reduce dementia symptoms and interpret any reduction as having "an effect" on dementia.

This behavioral symptoms definition of dementia is in contrast to the brain pathology definition of dementia, which the medical profession uses, and which focuses on identifying the parts of the brain where cognitive impairment originates.[7] However, let us initially begin with the medical definition of dementia and see where that lands us from a public policy perspective. Let us start with a list of the main types of dementia that the medical field have identified.[8]

- The most common form of dementia, comprising around 70 percent of the cases (the AA annual reports throughout the book are all based on US data), is Alzheimer's disease (AD). The pathology involves the outside of the neurons (the nerves in the brain) accumulating protein beta-amyloid plaques and inside the neurons, there exists twisted strands of the protein tau tangles. These plaques and tau tangles eventually damage and lead to the death of the neurons.
- The second most common form of dementia is vascular dementia. This is present in approximately 40 percent of the cases of dementia, as it is most often present in addition to other types of dementia. On its own, it exists in 10 percent of the cases of dementia. The way this disease works is to damage the brain by causing silent strokes (infarcts) or bleeding.
- Next, there is dementia with Lewy bodies (DLB). Lewy bodies are clumps (abnormal aggregations) of the protein alpha-synuclein in the neurons. Dementia often results when these proteins enter the cortex part of the brain (the outermost layer of the brain).
- Parkinson's disease (PD) is like DLB in that the protein alpha-synuclein also exists in the neurons, but for PD they accumulate in an area deep in the brain (in the substantia nigra) and not the cortex. The way this disease works is to damage the nerve cells that produce dopamine, which is a chemical that acts as a messenger between brain cells that affect how we move, what we eat, and how we learn. The main difference between PD and DLB is that the onset of disease with PD has motor impairment, while it is more cognitive impairment with DLB. The number of cases is about 10 percent of those with AD.

- Mixed dementia cases usually combine AD with either vascular dementia or DLB (or all three of these types). About half of all the persons with dementia have mixed cases.
- To complete this list of the main types of dementia, there are the much rarer categories including: fronto-temporal lobar degeneration, which affects neurons in the front and side regions of the brain; Creutzfeldt-Jakob disease that causes other proteins throughout the brain to misfold and malfunction; and normal pressure hydrocephalus that leads to fluid build-up in the brain, increasing pressure in the brain.

The problem with sticking to the medical definition of dementia is that, at this point in time, "current therapies do not prevent, halt or reverse Alzheimer's disease."[9] So the public policy conclusion would seem to be that nothing can be done today that will reduce dementia.

On the other hand, if we switch to the alternative definition of dementia that instead focuses on behavioral symptoms, we would reach an entirely different policy conclusion. What is important is whether ADL can occur, or recur, not whether there is present brain pathology indicating a particular type of medically defined dementia. For brain pathology is neither a necessary nor a sufficient condition for ADL to be affected. Some people with the brain pathology do not have symptoms, so carry on their lives as usual, while others have no brain pathology, but cannot carry on as normal. By utilizing a behavioral definition of dementia that focuses on symptoms, it is possible to consider a whole range of existing dementia interventions that have been found to be effective. It is now not the case that nothing can be done to impact dementia.[10]

An intervention is to be considered effective if it reduces any dementia symptoms that exist, irrespective of the dementia type that initially generated the symptoms. Since we are focusing on the dementia symptoms, and not the dementia type, in this book we will often be using the terms "Alzheimer's" and "dementia" interchangeably.[11] In the next sections we briefly survey the main interventions that been found to be effective for reducing dementia symptoms.

INTERVENTIONS

The two most commonly prescribed medicines for mild to moderate dementia are cholinesterase inhibitors (the main ones are Rivastigmine, Galantamine and Donepezil) and for severe dementia, there is Memantine.

These medications improve symptoms by increasing the amount of chemicals (called neurotransmitters) in the brain. However, the evidence summarized in the 2018 Report finds that the improvement in symptoms from these medications is limited in duration and varies from person to person.[12] So we can say that, at this time, what effective medical interventions that do exist have effectiveness that is short-lived and not generally applicable.

Existing Non-pharmaceutical Interventions

There are well-known non-pharmaceutical interventions that exist that follow the often-stated maxim, "anything that is good for the heart is also good for the brain." The three main non-pharmaceutical interventions are cardiovascular exercise guidelines, sleep hygiene strategies, and dietary modifications:[13]

- For adults under age 65 who do not have contraindicated medical illnesses, the World Health Organization recommends 150 minutes of moderate cardiovascular exercise per week.[14] "Moderate" exercise is defined by the American Heart Association as exercising at 50 to 70 percent of one's maximum heart rate for age.[15] For older adults age 65 and over, the time recommendations double to 300 minutes of moderate cardiovascular exercise per week (or 150 minutes of vigorous cardiovascular exercise). Exercise contributes to normalizing the neuroelectrical functioning of the brain. Balance training can reduce the risk of falls and thereby avoid brain injury that contributes to dementia symptoms. More sophisticated balance training (such as tai chi) improves executive functioning of the brain by affecting prefrontal lobe cortex motor fields.
- There is a strong role of deep restorative sleep for the prevention of Alzheimer's disease. What is important is the glymphatic system in the brain that essentially washes the brain during deeper stages of sleep. In this way, there is the removal of amyloid-beta plaque by-products characteristically seen in Alzheimer's. To help restore deep sleep, the interventions (called sleep hygiene) include: implementation of simple behavior changes such as developing consistent times to go to bed and wake up; avoidance of daytime napping of greater than 15–20 minutes; and leaving the bedroom if sleep onset has not occurred within 20 minutes.[16]

- A diet that contributes to weight loss is not necessarily a brain healthy diet. So, a diet was devised to prevent dementia called MIND (Mediterranean-DASH Intervention for Neurodegenerative Delay). Central to the diet were green leafy vegetables and berries. This diet was found to reduce the incidence of abnormal brain neuropathology and thereby the incidence of dementia. Longevity was increased by an average of four years or longer in persons who developed Alzheimer's while maintaining a healthy diet. For older persons who lived mainly on a fast food commercial diet, there was accelerated brain shrinkage, especially in the memory important hippocampus.[17]

There is an extensive literature confirming the effectiveness of these existing non-pharmaceutical interventions and this literature was also referred to in the 2018 Report.

New Non-pharmaceutical Interventions

Not covered in the 2018 Report are five recently published non-pharmaceutical interventions that also reduce the symptoms of dementia. These new interventions are:

- Years of education.
- Medicare eligibility.
- Hearing aids.
- Vision correction.
- Nursing home avoidance.

The focus of this book is to explain in detail how these five new interventions work, how they impact dementia symptoms, and what they contribute to a public policy understanding of how best to intervene with dementia.

Establishing Effectiveness

As with any type of intervention, the effectiveness of these new interventions in reducing dementia symptoms must be demonstrated. An important part of demonstrating effectiveness is to check that what one thinks is a reduction in dementia symptoms resulting from an intervention is, in fact, due to that intervention, and not due to something else. For example, say we have switched back from the MIND diet to our regular diet and find that the dementia symptoms have increased. We would want to know how much of the increase is due to the change in diet, and how much is due to changes in any of the other factors that are known to adversely affect dementia symptoms, such as a person's age. Changes in these other determinants, called "risk factors" by the medical field, need to "be controlled for" when examining the relationship between any intervention and the corresponding dementia symptoms.[18] We now cover briefly the main dementia risk factors that need to be included as controls in analysing the effectiveness of any dementia intervention.

RISK FACTORS FOR DEMENTIA

The four main risk factors for dementia that have been identified as having an effect on dementia, separate from the effect of any intervention that one is evaluating, are age, family history, the Apolipoprotein E gene (APOE) and gender.[19]

- Aging is a universal determinant of dementia; the older one gets, the more likely it is that dementia will occur. The prevalence rate of dementia (the total *existing* number of persons with dementia as a percentage of all persons in a specified age range) roughly doubles every five years over the age of 60.[20] In the USA in 2019, 5.3 percent of people between age 65–74 have AD. This rate increases to 13.8 percent for those aged 75–84, and becomes 34.6 percent for people age 85 and older. The incidence rate of dementia (the number of *new* cases of persons with dementia as a percentage of all persons in a specified age range) also rises sharply with age. In the USA in 2011, the rate was 0.4 percent for those aged 65–74; it was 3.2 percent for those aged 75–84; and it was 7.6 percent for those 85 and older.[21]
- While family history is not necessary for people to develop dementia, having a parent or sibling (a first-degree relative) with dementia makes it more likely that one gets the disease. Having a family history of dementia seems to have an impact somewhat separate from inheriting the APOE gene, which is also acquired genetically from one's parents.
- Everyone inherits one of three forms of the APOE gene, e2, e3, e4. Relative to e3 (which is the most common), e4 increases one's risk, and e2 actually decreases one's risk. Since one has two parents, and a person gets the gene from each parent, there are six possible pairs of gene combinations. Obviously, what produces the highest risk is the e4/e4 pair; 11 percent of the US population with AD have this pairing

and this increases the risk 8- to 12- fold (relative to the e3/e3 pair). Having just one copy of e4, which occurs in 56 percent of those with AD, increases the risk three-fold (again relative to the e3/e3 pair). This means that around two-thirds (65 percent) of US persons with AD have one or more copies of the e4 gene.[22]

- Worldwide, women with dementia outnumber men by 2 to 1. Some of this is due to aging, as women in the USA live 4–5 years longer than men. However, this is also because the APOE gene e4 that we just described confers greater AD risk in women than in men.[23]

These four risk factors have an influence on dementia separate from the effect of any intervention that one is considering evaluating. This makes them ideal from the statistical point of view for testing the effectiveness of any intervention in reducing the symptoms of dementia, as they are *not modifiable* risk factors. So, if one were going to estimate the effect of, say, diet changes on dementia, and one includes the risk factors in the estimation, one knows two things. Diet changes cannot affect any of the four risk factors (changing your diet cannot make you younger). Nor if dementia does change, because of the diet change, will any of the non-modifiable risk factors also change (reducing dementia does not make you younger). Including the risk factors in the estimation of any intervention ensures that one has isolated the real intervention's effect, as neither the symptoms nor the risk factors are changing *independently* of the intervention change. This means that any effect that one estimates of the diet change on dementia symptoms must be *net* of the effects of age, family history, inherited genes, and gender.

In addition to the four non-modifiable risk factors just identified, several *modifiable* risk factors also have been found to exist. Many of these involve the heart and therefore can be called cardiovascular risk factors for dementia. These risk factors include: obesity, hypertension, blood pressure, smoking, and alcohol consumption.[24] The complication here is that these risk factors, for many different sorts of reason, do have an impact on dementia that does vary with age (or any non-modifiable risk factor). For example, in late-life obesity has been associated with a decreased risk of dementia. One can immediately see some problems of including these modifiable risks as controls, or even treating them as interventions in their own right. To illustrate these problems let us focus on this negative association (correlation) between obesity and dementia often found in the literature.

First, as an intervention for dementia, encouraging obesity cannot really be the answer. Having a stroke and dying from it certainly reduces the chances of getting dementia, but killing people off is not what public policy tries to achieve. Moreover, the negative association between obesity and dementia has been found to have a simple explanation. People with dementia lose their appetite and thus lose weight (and become less obese). The negative association is simply reverse causation from dementia to obesity and not the other way around. Note that for any of the non-modifiable risk factors we identified earlier, reverse causation was ruled out. Dementia cannot reverse aging, so the relationship must be from aging to dementia and not the other way around.

Second, obesity could be correlated with any intervention that one is testing, so including it as a control would adversely affect the test one is undertaking to establish the effectiveness of the intervention. Let us again consider the MIND diet intervention. Switching to the MIND diet, as would be the case with any diet, involves reducing calories. Obesity automatically would go down. Given the inverse relationship between obesity and dementia, dementia symptoms would go up. Any negative effect of the MIND diet on dementia would be confounded with the simultaneously rising effect of dementia due to obesity falling. To be a good control variable in a test of any intervention, it is necessary that the variable remains unchanged when the intervention varies. This is why aging, which cannot vary when any intervention is changed, would be a good control variable and obesity would not.

Even if one can identify an intervention that has been estimated to reduce the symptoms of dementia, in the presence of the non-modifiable risk factors, and so its effectiveness has been established, it is important to understand that public policy has to be concerned with more than effectiveness. This is where CBA has a central role to play, as we now explain.[25]

THE ROLE OF CBA IN PUBLIC POLICY DECISION-MAKING RELATED TO DEMENTIA INTERVENTIONS

In addition to knowing an intervention's effectiveness, one needs to know whether that intervention is worthwhile, that is, worth devoting resources to, by the private and/or public (government) sectors. This is the public policy challenge for dementia interventions. The medical profession has been mainly concerned with the effectiveness part of this challenge. Obviously, there is no point in anyone devoting resources to an intervention that does not have any impact on dementia. However, once this hurdle has been overcome (and eventually a brain-changing, pharmaceutical intervention will most likely be invented), the next question is should an effective medical intervention be financed? Say a drug exists that can reduce dementia in a significant way by taking daily pills over a lifetime that costs $1 million per person, does it necessarily follow that $1 million should be spent on this medication?

The answer depends on the size of the measured monetary benefits of the reduced dementia.[26] If, for example, they have a lifetime value of $5 million then the expenditure on the drug is worthwhile, as the net-benefits, the difference between the benefits and the costs, is $4 million. That is to say, people are $4 million better off by having the drug. This is the CBA criterion for deciding whether to finance any sort of intervention, whether in the health care field or in any other areas of application. The net-benefits must be positive for an intervention to be worthwhile. Who pays for the drug has also to be determined by undertaking a CBA, whether it is the persons receiving the medications, a private insurance company, or the government. Nonetheless, irrespective of the method of finance, private or public, it is important from the public policy perspective that someone pays for the drugs if they make people better off.

Now assume that the lifetime benefits of the drug are not valued at $5 million, but are valued at $750,000. What would be the new verdict for investing in the drug intervention? Since the net-benefits are negative, equal to a loss of a $750,000, the $1 million drug investment would not be worthwhile. This conclusion holds even though the medications were found to be effective.

Testing for effectiveness is indeed necessary to be able to produce a favorable outcome. Note that, by definition, if something is ineffective then the benefits are zero. Ineffective interventions are always not worthwhile, as costs are positive and net-benefits must be negative. Therefore, the fact that an intervention is not ineffective inherently means that the benefits are positive. Therefore, the medical profession is right to check for the effectiveness of all dementia interventions. However, this is only the first step for an evaluation to reach a positive outcome. Costs are important too and these need to be estimated, so their size can be compared to the benefits.

Calculating the benefits of a dementia reduction can be useful even when they do not exceed the costs for an existing medical drug intervention. For the size of the benefits become the benchmark for finding a new drug. For example, let us return to the case where the benefits of reducing dementia significantly are $750,000 and the cost of the existing drug is $1 million. The pharmaceutical company knows that people will not be willing to pay for its existing product. This gives a financial incentive for the company to undertake research in finding a new drug. If the new drug is shown in a clinical trial to have a significant dementia reducing effect at a lifetime cost of less than $750,000, then the pharmaceutical company can go ahead and produce the new medication; but not otherwise.

So far, we have just been considering pharmaceutical interventions without considering the existence of non-pharmaceutical interventions. Even if a new drug can produce $5 million worth of benefits, at a cost of $1 million, the verdict need not be for people to buy the drug, if non-pharmaceutical interventions cost less than $1 million, or produce benefits greater than $5 million. Public policy requires that the benefits and costs of all effective dementia interventions be calculated to ensure that people purchase the ones that have the highest net-benefits. Only in this way can any particular intervention be judged the best.

We wish to emphasize that the use of the term "benefits" means that the outcome is being valued in monetary terms.[27] The costs of health care interventions are almost always expressed in monetary terms, as in market economies resources are usually supplied only if the consumers pay the input prices, whether they be in the private sector or public sector. With both outcomes and inputs of an intervention being valued in monetary terms, as benefits and costs, the two can be compared to see which is bigger, and hence decide whether an invention is worthwhile or not. Public policy relies on CBA because it is the only method of economic evaluation that relies on both benefits and costs.[28] CBA will be undertaken to evaluate all the new interventions that we will be presenting in this book.

SUMMARY AND CONCLUSIONS

Definitions are neither right nor wrong. Instead, the test for definitions is whether they are either more or less useful. If one sits on a flat, wooden surface supported by four legs, it can usefully be called a "chair," even though the furniture item was designed to be a table for holding objects and not persons. Therefore, we can say that using the medical definition of dementia in terms of brain pathology is not useful at this time. Medical interventions that can alter brain pathology do not yet exist. Sticking to this medical definition would mean that we would have to conclude that, currently, nothing can be done to intervene to reduce dementia. By contrast, if we define dementia in terms of behavioral symptoms, as we do in this book, then there are interventions that already exist and are effective. The main interventions that have been extensively researched and found to be effective are cardiovascular exercise guidelines, sleep hygiene strategies, and dietary modifications.

In addition to any of the effective dementia interventions that do exist, we need to recognize that there are non-modifiable risk factors that also have a significant impact on dementia symptoms. The four main ones are age, family history, the APOE gene, and gender. These non-modifiable risk factors have an important role to play in establishing the effectiveness of any intervention that one is testing. Including these risk factors in the estimation of effectiveness helps to ensure that the impact of any intervention on dementia symptoms is correctly measured. This is because, as the risk factors cannot change when any intervention changes, any dementia symptoms change can be interpreted as being the result of the intervention, and not some other influence. The role of these non-modifiable risk factors is therefore to act as controls in the estimation of the effectiveness of an intervention.

Other risk factors found for dementia that are modifiable, which include obesity, hypertension, blood pressure, smoking, and alcohol consumption, cannot be used as controls in the empirical estimation of effectiveness. These risk factors represent lifestyle choices. They can go up and down over time and this could coincide with any intervention change and thus confound the impact of any intervention. Although these modifiable risk factors cannot be used in the estimation of the effectiveness of an intervention for reducing dementia symptoms, as we shall see, they can still play a role in the estimation of the consequences of any change in dementia symptoms from an intervention on variables that matter to those with dementia. These variables include the quantity and quality of the lives of the people with dementia and caregiver costs.[29]

Once we know that any intervention one is considering has been found to be effective, the next public policy concern is to decide whether that intervention is socially worthwhile, and therefore an intervention that needs to be invested in. An intervention is worth financing if the monetary value of the outputs, the benefits, exceeds the monetary value of the inputs, the costs. In essence, a CBA examines all the advantages and all the disadvantages of a public policy intervention. By express- ing these advantages and disadvantages in monetary terms, one can obtain an overall assessment of the relative importance of each of the advantages and disadvantages. This is the role of CBA as it provides an economic evaluation of the intervention. CBA is vital to public policy decision-making as it recognizes that being a worthwhile intervention is more than being an effective intervention. The medical field has focused too much on trying to establish the effectiveness of a dementia intervention, at the expense of identifying interventions that are worthwhile and need to be financially supported.

The main purpose of this book is to present the results for five interventions, and their public policy implications, that are new (recently published), shown to be effective (in a causal way), and have been evaluated using CBA methods. These five new interventions are: years of education, Medicare eligibility, hearing aids, vision correction, and nursing home avoidance.

Given that we have adopted a behavioral definition of dementia, the outcome measure that we will be analysing is activities of daily living, ADL. We need to specify exactly what these activities require, and how the dementia symptoms that affect these activities are to be measured. All the five new interventions will use the same measure of dementia symptoms, and use the same data set. Explaining the dementia symptoms measure, and summarizing the data, is the subject matter of Chapter 2. Chapters 1 and 2 cover all the necessary introductory material for the book and this forms Part I.

Part II presents the CBAs of the five new interventions and they are contained in Chapters 3 to 7. Chapter 3 is on years of education, Chapter 4 is on Medicare eligibility, Chapter 5 is on hearing aids, Chapter 6 is on vision correction, and Chapter 7 is on avoiding nursing homes.

The last two chapters put all dementia interventions in a wider public policy context, and this constitutes the final part of the book, Part III. Chapter 8 covers elder abuse and Chapter 9 deals with human rights. Both of these chapters contain a CBA of a specific intervention using the same methods as for the new interventions in Part II. In this way, it is easy to see the unity in the content of Parts I, II, and III, and fully understand this book's central message. The message is that many types of effective dementia interventions already exist, they have been found to be socially worthwhile, and therefore merit fully investing in.

NOTES

1. The global dementia figures come from the *Global Action Plan on the Public Health Response to Dementia 2017–2025*. (2017), Geneva: World Health Organization; Licence: CC BY-NC-SA 3.0 IGO.

2. The US dementia figures come from Alzheimer's Association (2021), "2021 Alzheimer's Disease Facts and Figures", *Alzheimer's Dementia*, 17(3), 1–108.

3. A social evaluation involves valuing the effects of *everyone* affected by a policy or intervention. These effects may be for those directly affected, those indirectly affected, and third parties who have to pay taxes to finance the policies.

4. American Psychiatric Association (1994), *Diagnostic and Statistical Manual of Mental Disorders*, 4th edition, Washington, DC: AMA. In addition to the two cognitive deficits mentioned in the text, for dementia of the Alzheimer type, the cognitive deficits must not be due to other central nervous system conditions, such as Parkinson's disease and brain tumors, and the deficits cannot exclusively occur during the course of a delirium. The main other types of dementia are covered subsequently in the text.

5. Alzheimer's Association (2018), "2018 Alzheimer's Disease Facts and Figures", *Alzheimer's Dementia*, 14, 367–429. The quote is on page 5.

6. It is because behavior is intrinsically involved with the definition of dementia in terms of ADL that an economist has something to say about dementia and it is not just a medical field. Economics is all about explaining individual behavior in the context of making choices.

7. For a full discussion of the significance of distinguishing a brain pathological from a behavioral definition of dementia symptoms, see Brent, R.J. (2019a), "Behavioral versus Biological Definitions of Dementia Symptoms: Recognizing that Worthwhile Interventions Already Exist", *OBM Geriatrics*, 3(4), 2–14. doi:10.21926.

8. See the 2018 Report, op. cit., Table 1. Not listed in their Table 1, but covered elsewhere in the 2018 Report, is dementia caused by Traumatic Brain Injury (TBI). This occurs when the normal brain function is disrupted by a blow or jolt to the head or penetration by a foreign object. 1.7 million Americans sustain a TBI annually. The leading causes are falls, being struck by an object, and motor vehicle crashes. Not listed in their Table 1, and also not covered in the 2018 Report, is HIV-associated neurocognitive disorders (HAND). This is currently relatively rare in the USA, but it is already an especially important and increasing cause of dementia in Sub-Saharan Africa (SSA). The three types of HAND are: HIV-associated dementia (HAD); HIV-associated minor neurocognitive disorders (MND); and asymptomatic neurocognitive impairment (ANI). HAD is becoming less common and so ANI and MND predominate. There are around 8.1 million persons in SSA who have HAND; see Habib, A.G., Yakasai, A.M., Owolabi, L.F., Ibrahim, A., Habid, Z.G., Gudagi, M., et al. (2013), "Neurocognitive Impairment in HIV-1-Infected Adults in Sub-Saharan Africa: A Systematic

Review and Meta-Analysis", *International Journal of Infectious Diseases*, 17, e820–831.
9. 2018 Report, op. cit., page 62.
10. Brent, R.J. (2019a), op. cit.
11. Note that even though the data used to evaluate all the new interventions covered in this book come from the National Alzheimer's Coordinating Center, the data span all dementia types and not just Alzheimer's.
12. 2018 Report, op. cit., page 13.
13. The literature on these three interventions is reviewed in: Conder, R.L. Friesen, C., and Conder, A.A. (2019), "Behavioral and Complementary Interventions for Healthy Neurocognitive Aging", *OBM Geriatrics*, 3(1). doi:10.21926/obm.geriatr.1901039.
14. Physical Activity [Internet]. World Health Organization. Cited November 29, 2018. Available from: https://www.who.int/dietphysicalactivity/pa/en/ (accessed December 16, 2021).
15. American Heart Association. Cited March 1, 2019. Available from: https:// www.heart.org/en/healty-living/fitness/fitness-basics/target-heart-rates (accessed December 16, 2021).
16. Condor, R.L. et al. (2019), op. cit., page 5.
17. The MIND diet is explained and assessed in: Morris, M.C., Tangney, C.C., Wang, Y., Sacks, F.M., Barnes, L., Bennet, D.A., et al. (2015), "MIND Diet Slows Cognitive Decline with Aging", *Alzheimer's Dementia*, 11, 1015–1022.
18. As we shall see when we cover the new interventions in detail, a control is an independent variable that is included in any estimation equation, in addition to the intervention variable being tested, that is known to have a separate influence on the dependent variable one is trying to explain. In economics, almost any type of behavior can be partially explained by a person's age, gender, race, income, and education, and these would constitute the typical control variables.
19. Alzheimer's Association (2018), op. cit., pages 10 and 18.
20. Alzheimer's Disease International (2015), *World Alzheimer's Report 2015. The Global Impact of Dementia: An Analysis of Prevalence, Incidence, Costs and Trends*, London: UK.
21. Alzheimer's Association (2021), op. cit., pages 13 and 23.
22. Ibid., page 13.
23. Altman, A., Tian, L., Henderson, V.W., and Greicius, M. (2014), "Sex Modifies the APOE-Risk of Developing Alzheimer's Disease", *Annals of Neurology*, 75, 563–573.
24. Alzheimer's Association (2018), op. cit., page 11. The list of modifiable risk factors changed in Alzheimer's Association (2021), op. cit., page 14. The list was amended in line with the 2020 Lancet Commission on dementia. We analyse the 2020 Commission's recommendations in detail in the final chapter of the book.
25. For a simple introductory text to CBA for non-economists applied to many different types of intervention (health, education, transport, environ-ment, etc.), see Brent, R.J. (2017), *Advanced Introduction to Cost-Benefit*

Analysis, Cheltenham, UK and Northampton, MA, USA: Edward Elgar. For a more comprehensive text on CBA applied to just the health care field, see Brent, R.J. (2014), *Cost-Benefit Analysis and Health Care Evaluations*, 2nd edition, Cheltenham, UK and Northampton, MA, USA: Edward Elgar. For economists, there is a more advanced CBA text based on applied welfare economics, see Brent, R.J. (2006), *Applied Cost-Benefit Analysis*, 2nd edition, Cheltenham, UK and Northampton, MA, USA: Edward Elgar.

26. Measuring benefits basically involves putting a monetary value on (pricing) the outcomes from an intervention. There are many different ways of estimating the benefits for any intervention. The most convincing methods from a social perspective rely on advanced welfare economics principles; see, for example, Brent, R.J. (2006), op. cit. Note that we will return to the same issue (of evaluating a hypothetical effective drug), which we analyse now in this chapter.

27. Strictly, to be able to compare benefits with costs in order to calculate net-benefits, it is only necessary for benefits and costs to be measured in the same units. Almost all CBAs use money to measure the units for inputs and output. This is why this book defines benefits as outcomes in monetary units. For a CBA that uses time rather than money to value inputs and outputs, see Brent, R.J. (1991), "A New Approach to Valuing a Life", *Journal of Public Economics*, 44, 165–171.

28. Note that Cost-Effectiveness Analysis (CEA) is more often used than CBA in the health care field to carry out an economic evaluation. However, CEA does not tell us whether an intervention is socially worthwhile or not. An intervention can be the most cost-effective, and not worthwhile; and an intervention can be the least cost-effective, yet be worthwhile. For an example of the latter case, refer to antiretrovirals (ARVs) for HIV/AIDs. These drugs were shown to be the least cost-effective, yet still worthwhile when benefits were estimated – see Brent, R.J. (2011), "An Implicit Price of a DALY for Use in a Cost-Benefit Analysis of ARVs", *Applied Economics*, 43, 1413–1421.

29. As we shall see when we carry out the evaluations of the new interventions, the quantity and quality of the lives of the people with dementia, and the costs of the caregivers, will actually be the outcome variables that generate the benefits for the CBAs.

2. Measuring dementia symptoms

The 2018 Report explains that there are three discrete stages of dementia, only one of which is dementia proper (which we will refer to as "full" dementia).[1] For two of these stages, mild cognitive impairment (MCI) and full dementia, symptoms are present. For the other stage, preclinical Alzheimer's disease, although the brain has biological signs of dementia, there are no symptoms. As we explained, in Chapter 1, this classification system is not helpful from a public policy point of view. One can have no brain pathology of dementia, yet one can have cognitive interferences with activities of daily living, ADL, and one can have no cognitive interference with ADL even with the brain pathology of dementia. Therefore, what is important is whether one has symptoms, not whether one has the brain pathology of any particular designated category of dementia. We continue to use the words "dementia" and "Alzheimer's disease" interchangeably.

When having a reduction in dementia symptoms is the centerpiece for evaluating dementia interventions, as in this book, it is essential to have a quantitative measure of dementia symptoms. Although the 2018 Report gives many examples of dementia symptoms, in terms of significant problems with learning, thinking, or memory, what is strikingly missing from the 2018 Report is how to actually quantify these symptoms. Without a measure of dementia symptoms, how is one going to be able to know whether they are mild or severe, or have been significantly reduced? The contribution of this chapter is to describe and explain an instrument called the Clinical Dementia Rating scale (CDR), known as the *CDR® Dementia Staging Instrument*, created by Washington University to measure dementia symptoms. The CDR has been validated in the literature and allows one to monitor dementia symptoms quantitatively, in order that the impact of any intervention can be detected.

CHAPTER OUTLINE

It has been pointed out that we are all aging from the day we are born. The whole human body decays as we age. Even our brain shrinks with aging, so cognitive skills will also decline over time.[2] The challenge is to distinguish symptoms that are normal with aging, from symptoms that are abnormal with aging, which is the dementia disease state.

We start this chapter with an outline of the ten warning signs of dementia created by the Alzheimer's Association.[3] As a part of this account, a distinction is drawn between cognitive problems that are typical age-related changes, and those cognitive problems that are warning signs of dementia. This account serves as an introduction to the CDR, which although constructed many years earlier, can be interpreted to have taken the ten warning signs and converted them into six measurable symptoms of dementia. Once we have detailed the six CDR domains, we explain how they are to be aggregated to form the summary dementia symptoms measure for any individual, which is the CDR-SB (CDR Sum of Boxes).

After presenting the data source used for all the five new interventions, we use it to show how the CDR was distributed across the sample. Then we explain why the 18-point CDR measure is more useful for evaluating dementia interventions than the three discrete stages of dementia high-lighted in the 2018 Report. Next, we summarize an alternative measure of dementia symptoms, the 10/66 Dementia Research Group's criterion, which was devised to make the official DSM-IV dementia definition (explained in Chapter 1) more operational and relevant to developing countries.[4] We close the chapter by explaining why the CDR is more useful for our purposes than the 10/66 measure.

TEN WARNING SIGNS OF DEMENTIA

The Alzheimer's Association's ten warning signs for dementia are listed below in a slightly abridged form. For each sign, a description is given of what is somewhat abnormal (indicative of dementia) and what is some-what normal for someone who is aging.

1. Memory Loss that Disrupts Daily Life.
   - Dementia: Forgetting recently learned information, important dates or events, and asking for the same information over and over; increasingly relying on memory aids.
   - Normal: Sometimes forgetting names or appointments, but remembering them later.

2. Challenges in Planning or Solving Problems.
   - Dementia: Changes in one's ability to develop and plan or work with numbers; trouble following a familiar recipe or tracking monthly bills; trouble concentrating.
   - Normal: Making occasional errors when balancing a checkbook.

3. Difficulty Completing Familiar Tasks at Home, at Work or at Leisure.
   - Dementia: Finding it hard to complete daily tasks; trouble driving to a familiar location or managing a budget at work; trouble remembering the rules of a favorite game.
   - Normal: Occasionally needing help with microwave settings or recording a TV show.

4. Confusion with Time or Place.
   - Dementia: Losing track of dates and the passage of time; trouble understanding something not happening immediately; forgetting where they are or how they got there.
   - Normal: Getting confused about the day of the week, but figuring it out later.

5. Trouble Understanding Visual Images and Spatial Relationships.
   - Dementia: Having vision problems that lead to difficulty reading, judging distance and determining color or contrast, which may cause driving problems.
   - Normal: Vision changes related to cataracts.

6. New Problems with Words in Speaking or Writing.
   - Dementia: Having trouble following or joining a conversation; stopping in the middle of a conversation and having no idea how to continue, or repeating themselves.
   - Normal: Sometimes having trouble finding the right word.

7. Misplacing Things and Losing the Ability to Retrace Steps.
   - Dementia: Putting things in unusual places; losing things and not being able to trace the steps how to find them again; accusing others of stealing.
   - Normal: Misplacing things from time to time and retracing steps to find them.

8. Decreased or Poor Judgment.
   - Dementia: Changes in judgment or decision-making, for example, giving large sums of money to telemarketers; paying less attention to grooming or keeping clean.
   - Normal: Making a bad decision once in a while.

9. Withdrawal from Work or Social Activities.
    *   Dementia: Start withdrawing from hobbies, social activities, work projects or sports; avoiding being social because of changes experienced.
    *   Normal: Sometimes feeling weary of work, family, and social obligations.

10. Changes in Mood and Personality.
    *   Dementia: Mood and personalities can change; becoming confused, suspicious, depressed, fearful or anxious. Becoming easily upset in places familiar or new.
    *   Normal: Evolving specific ways of doing things; irritable when one's routine is disrupted.

Most of the dementia warning signs listed above form the basis for the CDR measure of dementia symptoms that we are now going to describe.[5]

THE CDR INSTRUMENT FOR MEASURING DEMENTIA SYMPTOMS

The CDR is a measure of dementia severity used globally based primarily on a neurological exam and informant reporting.[6] A CDR was administered by a trained clinician to each National Alzheimer's Coordinating Center (NACC) participant at each visit. The NACC is the data source for all five of the new dementia interventions highlighted in this book and this source is summarized below. The CDR has six components, called domains. The six domains are: memory, orientation, judgment and problem solving, community affairs, home and hobbies, and personal care. Memory corresponds directly with dementia warning signs 1 and 7, and orientation with sign 4. Judgment and problem solving is multifaceted and therefore spans signs 2, 3, 5, 6, and 8. Community affairs, and home and hobbies, are both related to sign 9 and personal care is a part of sign 8. There is no domain that *directly* corresponds to sign 10, mood and personality. Indirectly, sign 10 can be seen to be included in many of the CDR domains. For example, judgment and orientation may be hampered if someone is in a bad mood. But note that the explicit omission of sign 10 from the CDR domains may not be much of a weakness, given that the Alzheimer's Association qualifies sign 10 by pointing out that mood changes may also be a sign of other conditions than dementia.

Cost-Benefit Analysis and dementia

Table 2.1   *Clinical Dementia Rating scale (CDR)*

Impairment	None 0	Questionable 0.5	Mild 1	Moderate 2	Severe 3
Memory	No memory loss or slight	Consistently slight forgetfulness	Moderate loss; marked for recent events	Severe loss; new material rapidly lost	Severe loss; only fragments remain
Orientation	Fully orientated	Fully orientated except for time relationships	Orientated only for place at examination	Disorientated with time and place	Orientated to person only
Judgment and Problem Solving	Solves everyday problems; judgment good	Slight impairment in judgment	Moderate difficulty in judgment	Severely impaired in judgment	Unable to make judgments, solve problems
Community Affairs	Independent function at usual level	Slight impairment in activities	Unable to function at all these activities	No pretence of independent function outside home	
Home and Hobbies	Life and interests well maintained	Interests slightly impaired	Mild but definite impairment	Only simple chores preserved	No significant function in home
Personal Care	Fully capable of self-care		Needs prompting	Requires assistance in dressing, etc.	Requires much help

Source: The table is an abbreviated version of the one in Morris (1993), op. cit.

Most CDR domains are assessed using a 0 to 3 interval (none, mild, moderate and severe) with a questionable response being scored as 0.5. How the domains are scored is summarized in Table 2.1. We can see from the table that there are two exceptions to the usual scoring scheme. There is no "questionable" distinction for being fully capable of self-care in the personal care domain; and there is no "moderate" to "severe" distinction for the community affairs domain.

The CDR-SB is the aggregate score across all six domains and this has a range of 0 to 18. This will be the measure of dementia symptoms for all the CBAs. The aggregation is not as straightforward as it seems. The clinician is supposed to fill in the scores for each domain separately, except when they contradict the memory score that is considered primary and all other domains secondary. Therefore, for example, if the memory score is 1 or higher, the domain scores for a secondary domain included in the CDR-SB cannot be 0.[7]

THE NATIONAL ALZHEIMER'S COORDINATING CENTER DATA

The data that were used to carry out the CBAs of the five new interventions came from the NACC. The NACC has constructed a panel data set that has been operational since 2005, called the Unified Data Set (UDS). These data consist of demographic, clinical, diagnostic, and neuropsychological information on participants with normal cognition, mild cognitive impairment, and dementia who visited 32 US Alzheimer's Disease Centers (ADCs). In the latest version of the UDS there were around 35,183 individuals (clients) included, covering up to 12 visits per client, over a 13-year period. This data set is fully explained elsewhere.[8]

Although it is true that the UDS has been acknowledged not to be nationally representative, this does not necessarily mean that the sample was biased, with only those who think they have dementia visiting the ADCs. There were many other people involved with the decision as to whether a person shows up at an ADC. Some were recommended by ADC solicitation, some were referred by a relative or friend, and some referred by a clinician. The clinicians had a big say in who is included in the sample, not just the clients (for example, they ensured that the sample consisted of those with varying degrees of dementia, see Table 2.2). Once the sample was constructed, it was not the case that clients could select only what they wanted to answer. The clinicians also had a big say as to what questions were asked, and whether to accept a client's answer, for example, deciding whether clients being interviewed are capable of answering certain questions that involve judgment, such as assessing their quality of life (QoL). In addition, the client's accompanying informant had some input into whether the clinician should accept the client's responses as reliable or not.

A Summary of the CDR in the NACC Data Set

Table 2.2 gives a summary of the NACC data sample in terms of our measure of dementia. Just over a third of the sample did not have any dementia symptoms, which meant that two-thirds had some symptoms

Table 2.2   *Summary of the 18-point CDR-SB scale in the sample*

CDR-SB	Number	Percentage
0.0	12,743	36.22
0.5	3,782	10.75
1.0–1.5	3,799	10.79
2.0–2.5	2,664	7.58
3.0–3.5	2,170	6.17
4.0–4.5	2,306	6.55
5.0–5.5	1,793	5.09
6.0–6.5	1,155	3.28
7.0–7.5	710	2.01
8.0–8.5	521	1.48
9.0–9.5	512	1.46
10.0–10.5	531	1.51
11.0–11.5	412	1.17
12.0–12.5	466	1.32
13.0–13.5	229	0.66
14.0–14.5	185	0.53
15.0–15.5	156	0.44
16.0–16.5	193	0.55
17.0–17.5	183	0.52
18.0	673	1.91
Total	35,183	100.00

Source: The table is an abbreviated version of Table 1 in Brent (2019a), op. cit.

(or questionable symptoms). Since the average age of the sample was around 80 years, having a sample where most have some signs of dementia should be expected.

THE USEFULNESS OF THE CDR RELATIVE TO UTILIZING JUST THREE DEMENTIA STAGES

As we can see from Table 2.2, the CDR has 19 categories, excluding the 0-starting point. This means that there are 18 categories of dementia symptoms, a somewhat continuous range between 0 and 18.[9] Contrast this with the just three dementia stages listed in the 2018 Report: pre-clinical Alzheimer's disease, MCI, and full dementia. Let us try to assign the CDR categories to the three dementia stages. In the process, we will demonstrate the usefulness of relying on the CDR rather than the three dementia stages for evaluating dementia interventions.

In the CDR framework, 0.5 has a definite meaning, it means that at least some signs of dementia are present.[10] It seems straightforward therefore to assign the preclinical stage to the 0.5 CDR category. The problem then is how to set the CDR dividing line between the MCI and the full dementia stage. Note that it is only the full dementia stage of the three stages that is going to be how the 2018 Report wants to document the number of cases of dementia in the USA. According to the American Academy of Neurology, there are 15.8 percent of people in the USA over the age of 65 who have dementia. Summing the percentages in the last column of Table 2.2 from above the CDR category of 5.0–5.5 to 18 produces a sum of 16.84, which is close to the 15.8 percent US prevalence figure. This would mean that a CDR score of 6 and higher would correspond to someone being in the 2018 Report stage of full dementia.

Now consider what the challenge for a pharmaceutical company would be if a CDR score of less than 6 would be the target to have discovered a successful medication to reduce dementia.[11] A drug sold on the market that was able to reduce 1.91 percent of the population's CDR score from 18 to 9 would be judged to be a complete failure, even though these people's dementia symptoms were halved! With a score of less than 6 as the cut-off, any reduction in the CDR score, no matter how large, that did not end up below 6, would be judged a failure.

Clearly, using just one discrete stage to define dementia is not useful as a benchmark for judging the success of a reduction of dementia symptoms from any intervention (medical or otherwise) when one has available a more continuous instrument, the CDR. With just a 0.5 CDR reduction from 0.5 to 0.0 (never mind a 9-point reduction), 10.75 percent of the dementia population would be judged to be relieved from dementia symptoms. As we shall see when we go into detail with the five new interventions, a reduction just by 0.5 in the CDR score could be enough to have produced a successful, socially worthwhile dementia intervention.

THE 10/66 INSTRUMENT FOR MEASURING DEMENTIA SYMPTOMS

All five of the new interventions reviewed in this book used the CDR to measure dementia symptoms and this was based on NACC data that related to the USA. In the literature, there exists an alternative general measure of dementia symptoms, the 10/66, that was created to be more relevant for developing countries. The title of the 10/66 Dementia Research Group refers to the fact that 66 percent of all cases of dementia live in developing countries, while only 10 percent of the research into dementia is carried out in developing countries. The 10/66 Group was founded to remedy this research imbalance.[12]

The main issue was this. Since dementia is to be defined by cognitive disorders that interfere with ADL, there was a concern that the activities of daily living for a city-dweller in an urban city in a developed country would not be the same as a farmer in a rural area in a developing country. One of the tasks of the 10/66 was to highlight those differences and construct a dementia instrument that could be compared to the DSM-IV to see how large any differences were.

A key ingredient of the 10/66 measure is the Community Screening Instrument for dementia (CSI'D') established in 1993.[13] This comprised 36 components for the individual being screened, and 30 items for the informant accompanying the person being tested. There was a score for the individuals being tested, a score for the informant, and an aggregate score summing the individual and informant scores. The questions covered memory, abstract thinking, judgment, other disturbances of cognitive functioning, personality changes, and functioning at work and in social relationships.

To test whether the CSI'D' was multiculturally valid, the scores for two communities were compared: Cree-speaking natives living on reserves in Manitoba, Canada, and English speaking, non-Indian residents of Winnipeg, also in Canada. Cree is considered to be a spoken language. The interviews with the Cree was made on the assumption that many of the elderly would not be able to read or write. It turned out that the prevalence of dementia was estimated to be the same (4.2 percent) in the two communities using the CSI'D' measure. Comparable differences in scores for non-demented and demented individuals were found in both communities, thus validating the CSI'D' instrument. Since educational and cultural differences did not impact the CSI'D', it was an ideal instrument to use as a part of the 10/66 measure to test whether the DSM-IV was biased for developing countries.

In order that the DSM-IV could be compared with the 10/66 measure (partially based on the culturally neutral CSI'D'), the 10/66 group had to provide operational definitions for the components of the DSM-IV by, for example, specifying what was "memory impairment" and what was a "significant" decline in functioning. The resulting operational DSM-IV was found in Cuba to be less matched with trained clinician diagnoses of dementia than the 10/66 diagnoses, making the 10/66 a more valid instrument for developing countries than the DSM-IV.[14]

Using the 10/66 diagnostic criterion to estimate the dementia prevalence rate in the rural Hau district in Tanzania, the rate was 3.38 times higher than the prevalence rate estimated using the DSM-1V (21.6 percent versus 6.4 percent).[15] This result was consistent with other dementia prevalence rate studies for Peru, China, Cuba, Venezuela, and Mexico, which obtained rates that were 2–3 times greater than for the DSM-IV. The overall conclusion from the Tanzania study was that the discrepancy was mainly due to the underreporting of cases of MCI using the DSM-IV criterion. This is the main reason why the DSM-IV criterion was deficient in estimating dementia in developing countries. For full dementia cases, it was judged that the DSM-IV criterion was still the best standard.

THE USEFULNESS OF THE CDR RELATIVE TO THE 10/66 MEASURE

It is important to understand that we are not using the CDR to estimate the dementia prevalence rate. We are using the CDR to see whether any particular dementia intervention we are evaluating is effective and worthwhile. Nor does it matter that the MCI rate is better estimated in developing countries with the 10/66 than the DSM-IV. We do not need to use an MCI rate, as the CDR covers all gradations of dementia symptoms severity, not just mild; and the CDR has been shown to be valid globally, and not just in developed countries. For example, it has been shown to be valid in Brazil, Korea, Portugal, China, and Iran.[16] In any case, we are not relying on the DSM-IV, as the CDR quantitatively measures symptoms, while there is no specified instrument mentioned in the DSM-IV.

One further advantage of the CDR over the 10/66 is that it does not rely on a specific number as a threshold for defining full dementia, in addition to it not needing a threshold to define MCI. Although it would be easy enough to define full dementia as when the CDR is above 3 (more than one domain is present), or above 6 (more than two dimensions are present), or even above 9 (over half of the dimensions are present), we shall see that when the CDR is used to identify whether an intervention is effective or socially worthwhile, no threshold of any kind is required.

SUMMARY AND CONCLUSIONS

The 2018 Report states that: "It is important to note that not all people with MCI or people who are in the proposed preclinical stage of Alzheimer's disease will go on to develop Alzheimer's dementia."[17] So, what does it mean to say that someone who is without symptoms, and someone who never will have symptoms, is in one of three classified stages of dementia? Moreover, the dividing line between MCI and full dementia is that MCI persons may have many symptoms of cognitive decline, "but the individual is still able to carry out everyday activities."[18] Since not being able to carry out ADL is our behavioral definition of dementia symptoms, it does not make sense to say that MCI persons whose ADL can continue are in a dementia stage. Without an explicit measurement instrument that can cover all gradations of dementia, specifying three dementia stages as preclinical, MCI, and full dementia, as in the 2018 Report, is not very useful.

This then is the role of the CDR measure that we outlined in this chapter. It is an instrument for quantifying the symptoms of dementia that allows one to monitor them, over a specific range, somewhat continuously. With the CDR, it is now possible to quantify gradations of dementia, without requiring that only reductions in dementia symptoms sufficient to end up below some arbitrary threshold level constitute a successful intervention. On a scale of 0 to 18, even a 0.5 reduction in the CDR has meaning, no matter what the starting CDR level was. With a meaningful output, we now have a meaningful measure for which to assess the success of a dementia intervention.

In trying to measure dementia, it is important to understand that it is *changes* in the ADL that need to be monitored. Whether one pulls a plough manually in a developing country, or is driving a car in a developed country, the issue is whether these activities can continue as they are usually performed by the person involved. This is the reason why that, for all the dementia instruments covered in this chapter (the CDR, the CSI'D', and the 10/66), an informant (usually a close family member) accompanies the person while s/he is being tested for dementia. In this way, by listening to what the informant can confirm about the usual cognitive behavior of the person being evaluated, the clinician doing the dementia evaluation can check whether any current behavior is new or not.

The CDR shares in common most of the Alzheimer's Association's ten warning signs of dementia. What effectively distinguished a normal aging sign from an abnormal warning sign, and thus a symptom of dementia, was the frequency of the sign ("sometimes" versus "usually") and whether the symptoms were reversed (the cognitive problem was recognized by the person and then rectified before any interference in ADL resulted). The six domains of the SDR were measures of: memory, orientation, judgment and problem solving, community affairs, home and hobbies, and personal care. These six domains cover almost everything that is a part of daily living, in terms of what one thinks, what one does, where one goes, and whom one meets. What one feels or says is not directly included in the CDR; but they are included indirectly. Because what one feels or says will ultimately be manifest in what one thinks and does, and where one goes and whom one meets. If what one feels, or says, does not ultimately impact ADL, this can still be important to one's life; nonetheless, this is not dementia.

In the CDR, and all the other dementia symptoms instruments, together with the DSM-IV guidelines, memory is the most important ingredient in the overall assessment of the dementia outcome. Everyone forgets things occasionally. What a person without dementia can do, and someone with dementia cannot do, is recall at a later time what was forgotten, and also be aware that something was indeed forgotten.

It would seem that the CDR would have the drawback that because a clinician makes the diagnosis, it would be too subjective a measure of dementia. This would be unlike a diagnosis based on Magnetic Resonance Imaging (MRI), which is used to monitor brain activity. An MRI would show whether lesions, amyloid plaques, or tau tangles were present to confirm a pathological diagnosis of dementia. But, as we have tried to make clear a number of times: (a) if one cannot change what the MRI confirms, and (b) one *can* change what the CDR confirms, and (c) changing the CDR impacts our ADL, and thereby makes one better off, then (d) using the CDR is more useful than using an MRI to diagnose dementia.

With an understanding of the CDR-SB as the instrument for measuring the extent of changes in dementia symptoms, which is our measure of the output of an intervention, we are now in a position to explain in detail the CBAs of the five new dementia interventions. Because developing countries, that is, Low-and-Middle Income countries (LMICs), may experience dementia differently, for each new intervention, we will also discuss some of the implications of the US results for these countries.

NOTES

1. 2018 Report, page 15.
2. Gawande, A. (2014), *Being Mortal*, New York: Metropolitan Books, Henry Holt and Company.
3. Alzheimer's Association (2017), http://www.alz.org/10signs (accessed December 16, 2021).
4. The literature on the 10/66 measure is very extensive. We cite here just two of these publications that explain the methods and protocols of using the 10/66 instrument and summarize some of its implications and validation: Prince, M., Acosta, D., Chiu, H., Scazufca, M., and Varghese, M. (2003), "Dementia Diagnosis in Developing Countries", *The Lancet*, 361, 909–917; and Prince, M., Ferri, C.P., Acosta, D., Albanese, E., Arizaga, R., Dewey, M., et al. (2007), "The Protocols for the 10/66 Dementia Research Group Population-Based Research Programme", *BioMed Central Public Health*. Available from: http://www.biomedcental.com/1471–2458/7/165 (accessed December 16, 2021).
5. The NACC data set did also include an alternative measure of dementia symptoms to the CDR, consisting of the Mini-Mental State Examination (MMSE). The MMSE is simpler and quicker to fill in than the CDR is. It has a maximum score of 30 points for 30 correct responses to questions related to orientation (time and place), recall (immediate and delayed), attention (counting backwards numbers and letters), language (naming items, repetition, following commands, reading and writing), and motor skills (copying). A score less than 20 usually indicates cognitive impairment. However, the MMSE was available only in the later rounds of the NACC survey. So, using the CDR for our purposes has the advantage of allowing the full panel to be employed and this is the main reason why it was chosen as our dementia symptoms measure. Another reason for favoring the CDR instrument is that the MMSE has been found to have educational and possibly cultural drawbacks. For more on the issue of educational and cultural drawbacks in measuring dementia, see the discussion of the 10/66 instrument covered later in this chapter.
6. Morris, J.C. (1993), "The Clinical Dementia Rating (CDR): Current Version and Scoring Rules", *Neurology*, 43, 2412–2414.
7. In the full version of Table 2.2 that is in Morris (1993), op. cit., there are included at the bottom of the table a set of rules as to how to score the CDR-SB for all memory outcomes.
8. See, for example: Morris J.C., Weintraub, S., and Chui, H.C. (2006), "The Uniform Data Set (UDS): Clinical and Cognitive Variables and Descriptive Data from Alzheimer Disease Centers", *Alzheimer Disease and Associative Disorders*, 20, 210–216; Beekly, D.L., Ramos, E.R., Lee, W.W., Dietrich, M.E., Jacka, M.E., Wu, J., et al. (2007), "The National Alzheimer's Coordinating Center (NACC) Database: The Uniform Data Set", *Alzheimer Disease and Associated Disorders*, 21, 249–258; Weintraub, S., Salmon. D., Mercaldo, N., Ferris, S., Graff-Radford, N.R., Chui, H.C., et al. (2009), "The Alzheimer's Disease Centers' Uniform Data Set (UDS): The

Neuropsychological Test Battery", *Alzheimer Disease and Associative Disorders*, 23, 91.

9. Strictly, there are around 35 intervals of 0.5 units for the CDR and not 19, as 0.5 intervals are applicable to all 18 digits in the scale (except for the two cases mentioned in the text). Thus, with 35 intervals between 0 and 18, the CDR is very continuous over this range. Table 2.2 only presented 19 categories in order to ease the reader's visualization of the distribution of the CDR scores.

10. Supporting the interpretation that a CDR score of 0.5 is very meaningful is Morris's reporting that a score of 0.5 or more is associated with a diagnosis of AD that would come from studying lesions under a microscope (called histological), which was not the case for a CDR score of 0. See Morris, J.C. (1997), "Clinical Dementia Rating: A Reliable and Valid Diagnostic and Staging Measure for Dementia of the Alzheimer Type", *International Psychogeriatrics*, 9(Suppl. 1), 173–176.

11. In the text, we point out the problem of using a count of 6 as the threshold for defining full dementia when judging the success of a new medication for dementia. However, the same problem arises for any other discrete assignment of a number to the CDR for defining full dementia. See Brent, R.J. (2019a), where alternative threshold numbers are used to define full dementia based on the CDR distribution: Brent (2019a), "Behavioral versus Biological Definitions of Dementia Symptoms: Recognizing that Worthwhile Interventions Already Exist"" *OBM Geriatrics*, 3(4), 2–14. doi: 10.21926.

12. The 10/66 Dementia Research Group was formed in 1998, building a network of 30 research groups in 20 countries in Latin America, the Caribbean, India, Russia, China, and South East Asia.

13. Hall, K.S., Hendrie, H.C., Brittain, H.M., Norton, J.A., Rodgers, D.D., Prince, C.S., et al. (1993), "The Development of a Dementia Screening Interview in Two Distinct Languages", *International Journal of Methods in Psychiatric Research*, 3, 1–28.

14. Prince, M.J., Llibre de Rodriguez, J., Noriega, L., Lopez, A., Acosta, D., Albanese, E., et al. (2008), "The 10/66 Dementia Research Group's Fully Operationalized DSM-IV Dementia Computerized Algorithm, Compared with the 10/66 Dementia Algorithm and a Clinical Diagnosis: A Population Validation Study", *BioMed Central Public Health*. Available from: http://www.biomedcental.com/1471–2458/8/219 (accessed December 2021).

15. Longdon, A.R., Paddick, S-M., Kisoli, A, Dotchin, C., Gray, W.K., Dewhurst, P.C., et al. (2012), "The Prevalence of Dementia in Rural Tanzania: A Cross-Sectional Community-Based Study", *International Journal of Geriatric Psychiatry*, 28, 728–737.

16. Zadegby, N., Noroozian, M., Khalaji, H., and Mokhtari, P. (2012), "Validity and Reliability of Clinical Dementia Rating Scale among the Elderly in Iran", *Zahedan Journal of Research in Medical Sciences*, 14, 47–50.

17. 2018 Report, page 18.

18. Ibid., page 10.

PART II

The Cost-Benefit Analyses

3.   Years of education

In 2019, almost 80 percent of the US general public were concerned about developing dementia at some point in time, and one in four people thought that there is nothing that can be done to prevent dementia. Of health care practitioners, 62 percent also must have thought that nothing can be done to prevent dementia, as they thought that dementia is a part of normal aging (contrary to what we explained in the last chapter was different between normal and abnormal aging, such as the persistence of cognitive impairment symptoms).[1] In the context of public concern and widespread misunderstanding, a book revealing the effectiveness and social desirability of several new interventions for dementia symptoms may be particularly insightful.

We start our account of CBAs of new interventions for reducing the symptoms of dementia with the case of education.[2] The more years a young person has of schooling today, the greater will be the reduction of dementia symptoms down the road when the person reaches the age of 65 years and higher. In economics, education is known as "human capital" and as an investment it gives returns in many forms, generating higher incomes, lower criminal activity, and health benefits generally, for example, on average, educated persons live longer. All these benefits have been extensively documented. What is new to economists is the identification of education as an additional benefit category because it can reduce dementia symptoms.

Although the capacity of education to reduce dementia symptoms is not new to the medical field, our estimate of the quantitative contribution of education to reducing dementia symptoms, and a clarification of exactly why this occurs, should be informative. Part of the problem is that that the literature has found a large variation in the size of the education–dementia relationship. Our contribution here is to specify the "dose" of education that is most effective in reducing dementia symptoms.

CHAPTER OUTLINE

The starting point is to try to understand why the inverse relationship between education and dementia symptoms could be thought to exist. From a list of possible explanations, we will concentrate on two competing hypotheses that will be tested using our data. Distinguishing between these two explanations will be the basis of our strategy to ensure that we can justify giving a causal explanation for the inverse relation between education and dementia. Before we can evaluate the first of the new dementia interventions, we need to present the general framework to estimate the benefits we will be using for all the interventions that we will be covering. This general framework involves decomposing the benefits estimate into three steps. Using this general framework, one can clearly see the path from a change in an intervention to a change in the valuation of a social outcome that forms the benefits in our CBAs. We then apply the general framework to estimating the benefits of years of education. Since we pointed out in the last chapter that developing countries may experience dementia differently, we end the chapter by examining the relevance of our US findings of years of education on dementia symptoms for LMICs, focusing mainly on Sub-Saharan Africa.[3] We close with the summary and conclusions section.

OUR EDUCATION CAUSAL STRATEGY

There are five main explanations for why education is related to dementia symptoms:[4]

*   Brain reserve: A larger brain volume may produce a greater number of neurons or synapses (interconnection between the neurons) to mask the fact that brain pathology may have started and thus delay the symptoms of dementia. Coincidentally, because people with larger brain sizes are more likely to stay in education longer, this is how there is a relation between education and dementia symptoms, as they are both linked to brain size.
*   Cognitive reserve: Brain function and not brain size may be the link between education and dementia because with higher levels of education comes greater efficiency of neural networks. So as dementia-related pathology occurs in the brain, a greater reserve of cognitive processing is available, and this prevents the symptoms.

- The "use it or lose it" hypothesis: Lifelong cognitive activity may be necessary to help prevent cognitive decline, and those more educated may be more motivated to pursue intellectual stimulation over the course of their lifetime.
- The "brain-battering" hypothesis: Those more highly educated are likely to have a higher socio-economic status (the human capital income effect) and thereby live healthier due to greater access to health care and more advantaged lifestyles (for example, less exposed to toxins).
- Education is a proxy for third variables: Education could be a marker for innate intelligence, which could be related genetically, or environmentally, to other protective factors.

Of the five explanations, we will focus in this chapter on the first two explanations. Under the brain size hypothesis, education is not causal in any association with low education and high dementia symptoms, as it is brain size that is the common link. While in the brain reserve hypothesis, education is causal as it changes the structure and processing of the brain, such that it protects and provides resilience against any destructive pathologies that dementia brings. This limited focus on the first two explanations is consistent with the literature which just poses this dichotomy, does education affect dementia through neuroprotection (greater brain weight) or through the provision of greater brain resilience?[5] Note that with explanations three and four, education is still essentially causal. It is because people are better educated in the early years that they are stimulated to a lifetime of cognitive stimulation; and it could be because people are educated that their income and lifestyle improve.

As for the fifth explanation, that there is some third factor at play, this is the central estimation challenge for all the new CBAs in this book. That is, we must justify why we consider our estimation of intervention effectiveness for each new intervention to be convincing. We need to explain why any reduction in dementia symptoms can be interpreted to be the result mainly due to the intervention we are examining, and not due to its interaction with some other determinant that is a more fundamental influence.

Recall that we began to explain this issue in the opening chapter when we discussed the role of controls. There we listed various modifiable and non-modifiable risk factors, and used this list to distinguish variables that could be used as controls to test an intervention's effectiveness (the non-modifiable factors), from variables that could not be used as controls (the modifiable risk factors). Age was an example of a non-modifiable risk factor, and obesity was an example of a modifiable risk factor. Thus, age could be a control variable in estimating dementia, while obesity could not.

In terms of this chapter, dealing with using education as an intervention to impact dementia symptoms, the challenge for estimation posed by the fifth explanation is contained in the first explanation. The fifth explanation is saying that there may exist a third factor linking education and dementia; and the first explanation is saying that the missing third factor may be brain size. Hence, when we come to discuss our education estimation equation for dementia in a little more detail, we need to explain our strategy for ensuring that it will be cognitive reserve that causes the reduction in dementia symptoms, and not brain reserve. As we shall see, our causal strategy for education is simply going to be that we will control for brain size when we carry out our estimation of the effectiveness of education in decreasing dementia symptoms.

THE THREE-STEP FRAMEWORK FOR ESTIMATING THE BENEFITS OF AN INTERVENTION

We now set out the general framework for estimating the benefits that will be used for all our CBAs of new interventions. The benefits B for any dementia intervention can be estimated in three steps:

1. A given change in an intervention produces a specific change in dementia symptoms: *Change in Dementia* (CDR-SB).
2. The specific change in dementia symptoms produces a change in an output of something that society considers important: *Change in Quantity*.
3. The change in output is then given a *Valuation*, that is, a social price, expressed in monetary terms.

Combining the three steps, the complete benefit measure is:

$$B = [Valuation] \text{ of } [Change\ in\ Quantity] \text{ from } [Change\ in\ Dementia]$$
$$\text{from an intervention}$$

The first step involves a statistical estimation equation, with our CDR-SB measure of the change in dementia symptoms as the dependent variable, and the change in the intervention under evaluation as the main independent variable (with the control variables also included in the equation as independent variables).[6] This is the crucial first step that the medical literature has been most concerned with that involves establishing an intervention's effectiveness. If the coefficient attached to the change in an intervention is zero, then the intervention is ineffective, and the CBA has been completed. An inefficient intervention cannot produce any benefits, so there is nothing to offset the costs, so the intervention could not possibly be worthwhile. For an effective intervention, the coefficient attached to the change in an intervention must be non-zero, and negative if we want dementia symptoms to decline when the intervention gets larger. For simplicity, when we discuss the size of the coefficient for judging the effectiveness of any intervention, it will always be understood that we are talking about a negative number.

Recall that the last chapter was devoted to explaining that the Clinical Dementia Rating scale (Sum of Boxes) was how we were going to quantify dementia symptoms, and this could vary from 0 to 18. Even though it is true that for an effective intervention to exist the coefficient indicating how much the CDR-SB has declined must be non-zero, it is also true that the larger (more negative) this coefficient is, the more effective an intervention can be claimed to be. However, it is not in any way necessary that the coefficient be 18 for a socially worthwhile intervention to exist. This depends on steps 2 and 3 in the benefits measure. Before we cover steps 2 and 3, we need to note that in the last chapter, we explained that in the CDR framework, a 0.5 change has a definite meaning; it means that at least some signs of dementia are present. So finding a coefficient of 0.5 from step 1, denoting a 0.5 decline in the CDR-SB, should be considered the benchmark for a meaningful effective intervention.

Having observed some reduction in dementia symptoms from step 1, step 2 seeks to detect what it is of importance to people that that decline in symptoms changes. This is the change in quantity (of an output that is important) that is referred to in the benefit measure. Step 3 then seeks to ascertain in monetary terms what the change in the quantity that is important can be converted to. This is the valuation part of the benefit measure. We will be using different valuation methods for each of the five new interventions. Let us now explain how the three steps were estimated for the education intervention.

ESTIMATING THE THREE STEPS FOR THE BENEFITS OF YEARS OF EDUCATION

Step 1

Estimation of the effectiveness of education as an intervention was obtained from running a regression equation, with CDR-SB as the dependent variable on a list of independent variables, which included years of education and a set of controls.[7] The list of controls that were found to be statistically significant (not obtained by chance) were:

- Age (and age squared).
- Male (not female).
- APOE gene e4 (1 and 2 copies).
- Sibling with dementia.

As we know, the older one becomes, the greater the chances of dementia, and being male means that one is less likely to have dementia relative to females who are more prone. It is the presence of the APOE gene e4, and having a sibling with dementia, in the set of controls in the estimation equation for effectiveness, that is important in establishing causation for years of education in explaining dementia symptoms.

In the NACC data set, there was no direct measure of brain size (or weight) at birth. So, a proxy had to be found. It turns out that a group of researchers working on the ENIGMA project, established to analyse the many mental effects of brain size, found that brain size is more similar among family members than unrelated individuals.[8] Our proxy for brain size could therefore be hereditary factors, and this is what the variables APOE and sibling with dementia represent. To summarize the causation strategy: If, in the estimation equation determining dementia symptoms, we include hereditary factors as controls, together with years of education, one can be reasonably sure that the coefficient attached to years of education would be independent of brain size.

The results revealed that all the signs attached to the controls in the estimation had the expected sign. Aging increased dementia symptoms, being male decreased dementia symptoms, and the hereditary factors increased dementia symptoms. The coefficient attached to years of education was –3.609. Years of education lowered dementia symptoms considerably. To better interpret the size of this coefficient, one needs to be aware that years of education was measured on a logarithmic scale, which

Table 3.1   *Cost-savings benefits by year of education in 2010 prices (dollars)*

(1) Year of education	(2) Reduction in dementia (CDR units)	(3) Yearly benefits	(4) Discounted yearly benefits	(5) Discounted total benefits
1	3.1130	45,319	8,658	8,658
2	1.5565	22,659	4,459	13,116
3	1.0377	15106	3,062	16,178
4	0.7783	11,330	2,365	18,543
5	0.6226	9,064	1,949	20,492
9	0.3459	5,035	1,219	26,191
12	0.2594	3,777	999	29,377
16	0.1946	2,832	843	32,950
28	0.1112	1,619	687	41,787

Source: The table is an abbreviated version of Table 6 in Brent (2018a), op. cit.

has the result that the effect of a year of education was not constant, but varied with the number of years of education involved.

To see this clearly, understand that, with a logarithmic scale, the effect of a year of education becomes not just −3.113, but instead, −3.113 divided by the number of years of education. This means that for the first year of education, the CDR-SB declines by 3.113 points, which is a huge reduction since the CDR-SB is on a scale of 0 to 18, and we explained earlier that a 0.5 decline is meaningful. For the second year, it declines by 1.5565, that is, 3.113/2. This is still a considerable reduction, but not as large as for the first year. For 28 years of education, which is the highest number in the sample, the decline in dementia symptoms is 0.112. The reduction per year of education for a selection of years is presented as column 2 of Table 3.1.

Step 2

For the education evaluation, the change in output that is going to produce value, from the decline in dementia symptoms, is going to be the extent to which those experiencing the decline transfer from dependent to independent living. This is because dependent living is costly, in terms of caregiver time and resources, and there will be caregiver cost savings when a person moves to the lower cost independent living accommodation.

There were four levels of independent living in the NACC data set, corresponding to four different levels of caregiver costs:

1. Able to live independently.
2. Requires some assistance with complex activities.
3. Requires some assistance with basic activities.
4. Completely dependent.

The magnitude of the extent to which changes in dementia symptoms had on the level of independent living was obtained from a regression with the four levels of independent living as dependent variables, and changes in CDR-SB as the main independent variable. Age and race (being white or not) were the only significant controls in the regressions.

As expected, the estimation results showed that dementia symptoms reduce independent living and increase the three categories of dependent living. From every one-point increase in dementia symptoms:

- Independent living (level 1) goes down by −0.0686;
- Level 2 goes up by 0.0406;
- Level 3 goes up by 0.0181; and
- Completely dependent living (level 4) rises by 0.0100.

Hence, by education reducing dementia symptoms, we can reverse the signs and know how much education increases independent living and decreases the other three levels that are more costly.

Step 3

The final step in the benefit measure for the education intervention involves valuing (monetizing) the reductions in the three levels of dependent living brought about by the improvement in dementia symptoms. Based on a national longitudinal survey, there were estimates given of the costs of caregiving that were saved by the three reductions in dependent living:[9]

- Requires some assistance with complex activities: $13,188.
- Requires some assistance with basic activities: $27,789.
- Completely dependent: $28,501.

It was assumed that there were no caregiving costs for those now in independent living.

Combining the Three Steps

Let us now put the three steps into practice and estimate the benefits of years of education from reducing the CDR-SB. As stated earlier, the benefit measure is:

$$B = [Valuation] \text{ of } [Change \text{ in } Quantity] \text{ from } [Change \text{ in } Dementia]$$
$$\text{from an intervention}$$

To understand the complete method, consider how the benefits were estimated just for year 1 (all the other year benefits used the same method). We know from Table 3.1 that for the first year of education, the CDR-SB decline was 3.113. Let us trace out the cost saving from each level of dependent living that results in a per point decline in symptoms:

- Each point decline in symptoms led to a 0.0100 fall in completely dependent living (level 4) that saves $28,501. Therefore, the savings from the decline in completely dependent living was $285.
- Each point decline in symptoms led to a 0.0181 fall in level 3 dependent living that saves $27,789. So, the savings from the decline in level 3 dependent living was $503.
- Each point decline in symptoms led to a 0.0406 fall in level 2 dependent living that saves $13,188. This makes the savings from the decline in level 2 dependent living $535.

This means that for each point decline in symptoms the savings sum was $1,323. Thus, for a 3.113 decline in symptoms the savings for each year that dependent living declined was $4,118. Because avoiding dementia is expected to add 11 years to your life, the lifetime total benefit from the first year of education was $45,319. This figure is the first number in column 3 of Table 3.1. Each benefit amount in column 3 is calculated using the same method, recognizing that the decline in symptoms is going to be declining per year of education as given by column 2. The yearly benefits decline from $45,319 to $1,619 for the 28th year of education.

Now we have the bad news. Although the yearly benefits from education in column 3 look sizable, they occur in the somewhat distant future. Years of education in early years produce dementia benefits some 50 years later. In economics, future benefits are worth less than current benefits, not least because one can put current money in the bank and

earn interest. Which means that future benefits need to be discounted by
the rate of interest to be comparable with current day values. The relevant
social discount rate for the education evaluation was assumed to be 3
percent.[10] The current values for all of the yearly benefits in column 3 are
given in column 4 of Table 3.1.

The benefit values in column 4 are the incremental values per year
of education. The more years of education one has, the greater is the
cumulative total of the yearly benefits. The total discounted benefits for
all years of education are shown in the last column, column 5. We see
that one year of education gives discounted benefits of $8,658; and com-
pleting five years of primary education produces $20,492 of discounted
benefits. Completing high school after 12 years of education has $29,377
of discounted benefits, and this rises to $32,950 when completing college
after 16 years of education.

CARRYING OUT A CBA OF A SCHOOL DROPOUT PREVENTION PROGRAM

Although the dementia benefits in Table 3.1 of 12 years of education are
large, at $29,377, they would not (on their own) cover all the costs of
completing high school anywhere in the USA. However, an intervention
need not be an all-or-nothing endeavor and could be an incremental
adjustment. Consider a high-school dropout prevention program. One
devotes resources in a child's early years to generate future benefits in
many forms. For the Check & Connect school dropout program, the costs
were about $1,400 per student. For this investment, there was a 21 percent
increase in the probability of completing year 9.[11] If one completes year
9, one must have completed all the years up to year 9. In the table, we
see that the cumulative discounted benefits from 9 years of education are
$26,191. A 21 percent chance of receiving this amount is $5,500, which
is nearly four times greater than the costs. The school dropout program
was clearly socially worthwhile just because of the dementia benefits.[12]

RELEVANCE OF THE EDUCATION DEMENTIA BENEFITS RESULTS FOR LMICS

At first sight, Table 3.1 would seem to have immediate policy relevance
for low-income countries. In such countries, many older adults, when
they were young, either did not attend school, or attended school for very
few years. For example, in six villages in Hai district in the North of

Tanzania, for a random group of adults 70 years and older, 62.7 percent of females had no education at all, 30.7 percent had four years of education or less, and only 6.8 percent had more than four years of education. For males, the percentages educated were higher, but still very low by western standards, with 32.0 percent having no education at all, 49.4 percent having four years of education or less, and 18.5 percent having more than four years of education.[13] Since just a few years of education produces the largest reduction in dementia symptoms, a lack of basic education would therefore appear to be a major reason why dementia is so high in Sub-Saharan Africa (SSA). Intervening today by devoting resources to just a few years of early schooling would seem to be the best way of intervening to prevent future dementia.

It is therefore somewhat surprising that the relationship between education and dementia was judged to be "mixed" in SSA. While several studies did demonstrate an inverse association, some showed no relationship at all.[14] It is instructive to try to find out why in some cases there was no relationship. First, it mattered how dementia was measured in Hai, Tanzania. As we saw in the last chapter, the 10/66 measure was developed to improve on the DSM-IV measure. In Tanzania, there was a significant inverse relationship between dementia and education only if the 10/66 group measure was used based on their CSI'D' measure.[15]

Second, it needs to be made explicit that the results given in Table 3.1 should strictly be classed as being derived from years of *formal* education. Formal education is less prevalent in SSA. However, there exists informal and traditional systems of instruction that can be more suited to the environmental and socio-cultural demands in SSA. For example, in Hau, Tanzania, senior family members taught many children informally.

Third, gender was an important ingredient in the dementia–education relationship. In two cities in Central Africa, Bangui (Central African Republic) and Brazzaville (Congo), using the DSM-IV measure, primary education was significant for females, but not for males. Interesting, on its own gender was not significant (as it would have been in the USA) and, on its own, education was not significant (as it would have been in the USA). What was significant was the interaction between schooling and gender, that is, the significant variable was schooling multiplied by gender. The explanation given for this result was tied to the second point just made, in terms of the role of informal education. In this case, the informal education was being supplied by the occupation that men obtain that is not available to women. The explanation was that men are probably less affected by a lack of formal education because their occupational activities allowed them to compensate for it as they aged, which was not the case for women who usually worked at home. Domestic activities for women were judged to be not sufficiently stimulating.[16]

A final explanation we mention here for why the education-dementia link was found to be mixed in SSA is because the quality of a year of education is also mixed in SSA. Economists working on education in developing countries at the World Bank have recently recognized that the quality of education, and not just the quantity of education, is important. These development economists have come up with a new measure of education called the Learning-Adjusted Years of Schooling (LAYS). This measure combines years of schooling with test scores that record how much learning takes place at schools. To appreciate that the education quality component is important, and not just quantity, consider this one example. In Nigeria, 19 percent of young adults who completed only primary education are able to read, while in Tanzania this same category had 80 percent who were literate.[17] Years of education in SSA may not be a good measure of education for some low-income countries, and this could mask the real dementia–education inverse relationship.

SUMMARY AND CONCLUSIONS

In this chapter, we covered the first of the CBAs of new interventions that involved years of education. We presented the general framework for estimating the benefits for any dementia intervention that will be used for all the CBAs in this book. This framework involved three steps. First, an intervention needed to reduce dementia symptoms and, in this way, become classed as an "effective" intervention. Next, the reduction in symptoms following the intervention must affect something that people care about and thus provide value. Finally, a value (a price) must be assigned to the output change that is considered valuable. Combining the three steps produces the monetary estimate of the benefits of any intervention.

In the case of the education intervention, years of education were extremely effective. Just one year reduced dementia symptoms by 3.113 points, when the CDR-SB scale had a maximum of 18 points. Although years of education did have diminishing returns, it was still the case that five years of primary education would reduce dementia symptoms in total by 7.1081 points. Completing 12 years of education by finishing high school leads to a 9.6626-point total reduction in dementia symptoms. Any medication that could halve dementia symptoms would universally be classed as a "miracle drug." The education equivalent of this medication can simply be called "completing high school."

For the second step for estimating education benefits, the output that generated value was promoting independent living, and thereby saving the caregiving costs of dependent living.

The third step, requiring that a monetary figure be assigned to the output change, was straightforward in the education case, as market prices exist for each gradation (level) of dependent care support.

The bad news was that all the estimated education benefits that accrue can only be experienced far (more than 50 years) into the future, when the schooled person becomes an older adult, who then would have otherwise had dementia symptoms. Still, even allowing for the fact that benefits accrue in the future by discounting at a rate of 3 percent, discounted benefits were sizable, equal to $8,658 for one year of education, equal to $20,492 for five years of education, and $29,377 for 12 years of education. To highlight the fact that the estimated benefits were meaningful, an illustrative possible intervention was the evaluation of a dropout prevention program. By preventing somebody at school from dropping out by year 9, the benefits were nearly four times the costs. Such a program would therefore have been very socially worthwhile.

The contribution of this chapter to economists is that it shows that years of education could be added as a new category to the well-documented list of human capital benefits of education. The contribution that this chapter makes to the medical field is that our results help answer three basic questions about education and dementia. First, it answers the question as to what the appropriate "dose" of education is. Some medical studies specify "at least primary" or "some secondary" when relating education to dementia. Should "some tertiary" be the education specification? Using discrete categories is not as useful as our specification of education in terms of years of education that is a more continuous construct.[18] Our answer is that each year of education has its own impact. Table 3.1 can be referred to in order to answer any question about the effective dose of education.

Second, a question was raised about whether the effects of education on dementia were causal or not. The question being asked was whether education alters the brain pathology of dementia (is it protective?) or does it enable someone to manage the brain pathology better (does it provide cognitive reserve?). Brain size was a factor supplying greater neurons that aids brain pathology, and thus brain size was inversely related to dementia symptoms. In addition, because brain size and years of education are positively associated, this could be the reason education and dementia were inversely related. If this is true, education should not be classed as causal. However, in our estimation equation of education's effectiveness in reducing dementia symptoms we could control for the effect of brain size, since brain size was largely hereditary and we had hereditary variables included as controls. We could therefore confirm that years of education was indeed causal in the education–dementia relationship.[19] It was important that we found that education was causal by providing brain reserve, because if it were brain size that generated the reduction in dementia symptoms, education would not be an intervention that public policy could use. Enhancing nutrition would then be the relevant intervention because this is known to affect brain size.

Third, we can answer the question as to whether education was socially worthwhile or not. Years of education produced sizable monetary benefits. The size of the benefits was not sufficient, on their own, to finance all the costs that are involved in a child or student attending school. But, if an intervention entails making a change in school attendance possible, like a school dropout prevention program, then the measured benefits would greatly exceed the costs, making the education program intervention socially worthwhile.

When trying to apply our US results to SSA countries, we acknowledge that years of schooling corresponds just to years of formal education, and that cognitive reserve can be supplied informally outside the school setting by senior family members, or by occupational mental stimulation, especially for males. However, formal education should still be particularly effective in reducing dementia symptoms in SSA countries. This is because of how many fewer years of schooling these countries experience relative to the USA, and we found that the lower the number of years of schooling, the greater the effectiveness of each year in reducing dementia symptoms. When results in SSA do not confirm that education lowers dementia, it could be because one has not controlled for the quality of education.

Now that we have found that years of schooling is a causal factor reducing dementia symptoms, we can include it as a control in estimating the effectiveness for all the other new interventions that we will be detailing in subsequent chapters. We also found that age and gender were significant controls that would have general applicability. In this way, our work is consistent with the literature which states that: "Socio-demographic characteristics (like sex, age and educational level) are the minimum set of covariates that should be controlled for in the analysis, since these are determinants of dementia risk, and may well be associated with other potential risk factors."[20] To this minimum list must be added hereditary factors, chief of which is APOE e4, which we outlined in the last chapter, and now have found to be significant in estimating education effectiveness.

NOTES

1. Alzheimer's Disease International (2019), *World Alzheimer's Report 2019, Attitudes to Dementia.*
2. This chapter covers the CBA in: Brent, R.J. (2018a), "The Value of a Year's General Education for Reducing the Symptoms of Dementia", *Applied Economics*, 50, 2812–2823.
3. According to the World Bank, in 2018, a low-income country had a Gross National Income of less than $1,025 per capita, and most of the low-income countries reside in SSA; see the World Bank Atlas Method, https://datahelpdesk.worldbank.org (accessed December 16, 2021).
4. Alzheimer's Disease International (2014), *World Alzheimer's Report 2014. Dementia and Risk Reduction: An Analysis of Protective and Modifiable Factors*. See box 2.1 on page 17. There is a sixth explanation given in the box, called "ascertainment bias," whereby people who are better educated are more proficient at performing tests, which would include cognitive tests. So educated persons here would artificially appear to be less affected by dementia than they really are. We ignore this measurement error explanation category because, in our data set, it is experienced and trained clinicians who make the assessment of dementia symptoms. Therefore, the educated patients are less able to hide their dementia from these evaluators by their test taking abilities.
5. See, for example, Brayne, C., Ince, P.G., Keage, H.A.D., McKeith, I.G., Matthews, F.E., et al. (2010), "Education, the Brain, and Dementia: Neuroprotection or Compensation?", *Brain Imaging and Behavior*, 133, 2210–2216.
6. The estimation equation also includes a random error term to allow for the possibility that some influences may just be due to chance.
7. The full statistical specification of the dementia symptoms regression is equation (2) in Brent (2018a), op. cit., and all the estimation results are in Table 3. For step 2 in the estimation of benefits, the specification of the independent living regression is equation (3) and the estimation results are in Table 4.
8. Thompson, P.M., Stein, J.L., Medland, S.E., Hibar, D.P., Vasquez, A.A., Renteria, K.E., et al. (2014), "The ENIGMA Consortium: Large-Scale Collaborative Analyses of Neuroimaging and Genetic Data", *Brain Imaging and Behavior*, 8, 153–182.
9. Hurd, M.D, Martorell, P., Delavande, A., Mullen, K.J., and Langa, K.M. (2013), "Monetary Costs of Dementia in the United States", *New England Journal of Medicine*, 368, 1326–34.

10. A social discount rate of 3 percent was the recommended rate to be used for all economic evaluations in the USA; see Gold, M.R., Siegel, J.E., Russell, L.B., and Weinstein, M.C. (1996), *Cost-Effectiveness in Health and Medicine*, New York: Oxford University Press.

11. Tyler, J.H., and Lofstrom, M. (2009): "Finishing High School: Alternative Pathways and Dropout Recovery", *America's High School*, 19, 77–103.

12. In Brent R.J. (2018a), op. cit., a more conservative interpretation of "completing year 9" was assumed. The benefits were taken to apply only to year 9, which produced discounted benefits of $1,219. A 21 percent probability of obtaining this benefit would work out to be $256, which would not cover, by itself, the $1,400 costs. But, it would still be 18 percent of the costs, and note that dementia is just one, and probably the smallest, of the benefits of a pre-school program that have been estimated by economists to be very much higher than the costs. See, for example, Heckman, J.J., Moon, S.H., Pinto, R., Savelyev, P.A., and Yavitz, A. (2010), "The Rate of Return to the High/Scope Perry Preschool Program", *Journal of Public Economics*, 94, 114–128.

13. Paddick, S-M., Longdon, A.R., Gray, W.F., Dotchin, C., Kisoli, A., and Walker, R. (2014), "The Association between Educational Level and Dementia in Rural Tanzania", *Dementia & Neuropsychologia*, 8, 117–125.

14. For example, see Ogunniyi, A., Hall, K.S., Gureje, O., Baiyewu,O., Gao, S., Unverzagt, F.W., et al. (2006), "Risk Factors for Incident Alzheimer's Disease in African Americans and Yoruba", *Metabolic Brain Disorders*, 21, 235–240.

15. Paddick, S-M., Longdon, A.R., Kisoli, A., Dotchin, C., Gray, W.K., Dewhurst, F., et al. (2013), "Dementia Prevalence Estimates in Sub-Saharan Africa: Comparison of Two Diagnostic Criteria", *Global Health Action*, April 3; 6: 19646. doi: 10.3402/gha.vi0.19646.

16. Guerchet, M., Mouanga, A.M., M'belesso, P., Tabo, A., Bandzouzi, B., Paraïso, N., et al. (2012), "Factors Associated with Dementia among Elderly People Living in Two Cities in Central Africa: The EDAC Multicenter Study", *Journal of Alzheimer's Disease*, 28, 15–24.

17. Filmer, D., Rogers, H., Angrist, N., and Sabarwal, S. (2018), "Learning Adjusted Years of Schooling (LAYS): Defining a New Macro Measure of Education", Policy Research Working Paper 8591, World Bank Group, Washington, DC.

18. The use of discrete categories for education has been attributed to be the main reason why studies of the education–dementia relation have obtained such variable quantitative results. As Alzheimer's Disease International (2014), op. cit., page 23, states: "Lower levels of education appear to be consistently associated with an increased incidence of dementia, with heterogeneity among studies largely relating to variability in the size, rather than the direction of the association. This heterogeneity may well arise from the relatively crude and variable nature of the dichotomized (low vs. high) education exposure." To illustrate the fact that one can be completely misled by focusing on a dichotomized classification of education in the context of intervening for dementia, consider this summary of the literature by Sanjay

Gupta on the role of higher education (college attendance and advanced degrees). See his book, Gupta, S. (2020), *Keep Sharp: Build a Better Brain at Any Age*, New York: Simon & Shuster. On page 119 of his book, he writes: "the long-held theory that a college education will fend off dementia later in life has been debunked as a result of a 2019 study published in the journal *Neurology*." He adds, "these results did not show a relationship between a higher level of education and a slower rate of decline of thinking and memory skills or a later onset of the accelerated decline as dementia starts." The problem here is that the focus is only on the level "higher education" and not years of education as a more continuous variable. Refer back to Table 3.1 (or ideally the full table for all 28 years of education in Brent, 2018a). The main point is simply that there are decreasing returns to years of education. Year 1 gives a 3.113-point reduction in dementia symptoms, while the last year of a four-year college, year 16, only produces a 0.1946-point reduction. Compared to all the years before higher education, which is years 1 to 12, the years 13 to 16 are bound to produce a lower decline, so relatively higher education is less productive. Therefore, this in no way negates ("debunks") the central finding in Brent (2018a) that all years of education help to reduce dementia symptoms later in life, even those in higher education.

19. Our finding that education is causal in the education–dementia relation should not be surprising. As Alzheimer's Disease International (2014), op. cit., page 18, states: "Cognitive Reserve has become the dominant explanatory framework for education and risk of dementia, to the point where education is now widely used as a proxy for Cognitive Reserve."
20. Alzheimer's Disease International (2014), op. cit., page 8.

4. Medicare eligibility

We have just seen that the costs of caregivers in non-independent living could be used as a measure of the benefits of an education intervention for dementia symptoms. This was because years of education reduced dementia symptoms, which promoted independent living, and this produced caregiver cost savings. Now for the CBA of Medicare eligibility, we consider the flip side to costs, which is that extra costs mean that usually extra services are being provided. With extra services comes an increased quality of life (QoL) for those with dementia symptoms, and in this way a more direct category of benefits comes into play in the evaluation of interventions.[1]

When extra services are being supplied, these services need to be financed by someone. In the last chapter, when independent living was involved, the private sector was doing most of the financing and receiving most of the benefits from the dementia reduction. In this chapter, we will be turning our attention to the public sector's involvement in the finance of services for those with dementia symptoms, in the form of the US health insurance program for older adults, called Medicare. People with dementia account for 64 percent of Medicare beneficiaries living in a nursing home.[2]

CHAPTER OUTLINE

We will still be using cost savings to caregivers from the transfer to independent living, because of the reduction in dementia symptoms, as the measure of benefits. The difference is that the transfer will be larger now because of the increased QoL following from Medicare eligibility. As part of our introduction to Medicare, we list some of the services that Medicare provides to people with dementia. The question then is, with all the extra services provided by Medicare to those with dementia, to what extent do they increase the QoL of those with dementia? To help us answer this question we need a quantitative measure for the QoL. For persons with dementia in our data set, the Geriatric Dementia Scale (GDS) short form will be this instrument.[3] After summarizing the

GDS, we explain the causal strategy for establishing the effectiveness of Medicare eligibility for reducing dementia symptoms. Then we proceed to carry out the three-step procedure for benefits that will be used in the CBA evaluating Medicare eligibility. When the CBA is completed, we will discuss whether there are any lessons to be learned from this US experience for LMICs. We close with the summary and conclusions section.

MEDICARE'S FOUR PARTS AND HOW THEY RELATE TO DEMENTIA SERVICES

Medicare is a national US health insurance program for people 65 and older.[4] The program is divided into four parts and was started in 1965. Initially, coverage was limited to part A. Coverage has evolved over the years with the final part D rolled out in 2006. Around 56 million people now have coverage with Medicare. The main parts, and how they relate to services for patients with dementia, are listed below.

Part A

This covers the cost of inpatient care and skilled nursing facilities (SNF) stays.[5] It helps with home health care only if carried out by skilled nurses. The coverage is basically for "room and board" in the hospital, as part A does not cover any treatments in hospital such as scans and surgeries. On the whole, nursing homes (NH) and long-term care are not covered, except when a person needs to be transferred from assisted living or an NH into a hospice (when a doctor certifies that life expectancy is six months or less).[6]

- Medicare coverage for emergency hospital care is especially important for people with dementia. Between 37 and 54 percent of people with dementia visited the emergency room (ER) in any given year, relative to between 20 and 31 percent of individuals without a dementia diagnosis. A large study found that average ER Medicare payments for patients with dementia (at any time during the 11-year study period) were 75 percent higher than for patients without dementia ($6,028 vs. $3,454). These Medicare cost findings persisted after adjustment for age, race, gender, and number of comorbidities.[7]

Part B

This pays for outpatient care, which is basically all the needs outside the inpatient hospital setting. Thus, the main elements would be doctors' visits (including those in hospital) and preventative services.

- Since dementia is a progressive rather than an acute disease, most dementia care claims will fall under part B. Medicare will usually pay for dementia assistance if a physician considers it medically necessary (and accepts Medicare coverage). An Annual Wellness Visit (AWV) is provided for everyone on Medicare. As part of an AWV, a cognitive assessment is carried out for older adults. The doctor may order diagnostic testing to view abnormalities in the brain. Another covered benefit is occupational therapy to improve cognitive function, which is called cognitive rehabilitation (and covered in the final chapter, Chapter 9).

Part C

Since parts A and B both have deductibles and copayments (for example, part B only covers 80 percent of one's outpatient costs), part C is designed to insure some of the gaps in coverage by supplementing the other parts. There is a choice of plans with various cost-sharing options. The government plan C is called Medigap, and the private sector part C is called Medicare Advantage.

- As part C is an optional plan that depends on a person's willingness and ability to pay for extra coverage there are no explicit provisions favoring dementia patients.

Part D

This is the newest provision that covers prescription medicines.

- Although the two main classes of anti-dementia pharmaceutical medications identified in Chapter 1 did not provide long-lasting improvement, they did ease dementia symptoms somewhat in the short term. Therefore, covering the cost of these medications did have some advantages for those with dementia. The result of including drug coverage as part D in 2006 was a relatively large increase in the use of anti-dementia medications. Even when the numbers who previously used part C to supplement their purchases of the drugs were included, and not just those with no coverage prior to 2006, the proportion of individuals using anti-dementia drugs increased from 2.4 percent in 2004 to 5.3 percent in 2007.[8]

We see from this brief introduction to Medicare that there are several different types of service that could potentially increase the quality of life for those with dementia symptoms.

THE GERIATRIC DEPRESSION SCALE AS THE MEASURE OF QUALITY OF LIFE[9]

The QoL measure that is in the NACC data set that we will be using as a negative proxy for utility is the Geriatric Depression Scale (GDS), short form. Although the GDS was originally conceived to be a measure of psychological status, it has become accepted as a valid measure of QoL among the elderly with and without cognitive impairment. For example, when reviewing the literature concerning whether physical activity improves the QoL of the elderly, the GDS was classed as one of the "measurement instruments most commonly used" to record the QoL.[10]

Table 4.1 identifies all 15 of the components that make up the total GDS. Each component is scored on a 0 to 1 scale, according to whether the response is "no" or "yes." Whether the score is 0 or 1 depends on whether the answer is averse to their QoL (for a score of 1) or the answer is positive to their QoL (for a score of 0). Thus, GDS1 is scored 1 if the answer is no, individuals are not satisfied with their lives; and GDS2 is scored 1 if the answer is yes, individuals have dropped doing many of their activities and interests. The logic of the scoring is that when one adds the 1s, one is always moving in the same direction of an averse QoL assessment. This means that the total GDS score, which is the sum of the 1s for the 15 ingredients, and is going to be our measure of QoL in our work, is a negative proxy for QoL. In our data set, the average total GDS score was at the low end equal to 1.96 (though some persons did have the maximum score of 15).

That the GDS is an appropriate measure of QoL can be seen directly from two of its constituent ingredients, which ask whether patients are basically "satisfied with their life" (GDS1) and whether they "feel happy most of the time" (GDS7). Often these happiness and satisfaction measures are the sole ingredient of a QoL index used in economics.[11] Our use of the GDS for our data set may be seen to be reliable because there is

Cost-Benefit Analysis and dementia

Table 4.1   *Geriatric Depression Scale (GDS)*

GDS Ingredient	GDS Question	GDS Score
GDS1	Are you basically satisfied with your life?	Yes = 0, No = 1
GDS2	Have you dropped many of your activities and interests?	Yes = 1, No = 0
GDS3	Do you feel that your life is empty?	Yes = 1, No = 0
GDS4	Do you often get bored?	Yes = 1, No = 0
GDS5	Are you in good spirits most of the time?	Yes = 0, No = 1
GDS6	Are you afraid that something bad is going to happen to you?	Yes = 1, No = 0
GDS7	Do you feel happy most of the time?	Yes = 0, No = 1
GDS8	Do you often feel helpless?	Yes = 1, No = 0
GDS9	Do you prefer to stay at home, rather than going out and doing new things?	Yes = 1, No = 0
GDS10	Do you feel you have more problems with memory than most?	Yes = 1, No = 0
GDS11	Do you think it is wonderful to be alive now?	Yes = 0, No = 1
GDS12	Do you feel pretty worthless the way you are now?	Yes = 1, No = 0
GDS13	Do you feel full of energy?	Yes = 0, No = 1
GDS14	Do you feel that your situation is hopeless?	Yes = 1, No = 0
GDS15	Do you think that most people are better off than you are?	Yes = 1, No = 0

Source: Constructed by the author based on Sheikh and Yesavage (1986), op. cit.

a clinician interviewing the patient who decides whether the person is, or is not, able to complete the GDS rating. Irrespective of the severity of dementia, it was found that around 95 percent of the persons whose competence was assessed by the clinicians were capable of completing the GDS scale in our data set.

OUR MEDICARE CAUSALITY STRATEGY

Establishing causality for Medicare was always going to be a difficult challenge. When economists first looked at the data relating Medicare and health care expenditures, they came across this problem when trying to interpret existing data.[12] Prior to Medicare eligibility at the age of 65, persons as they age would have a gradual increase in use of health care services. Then as soon as people turn 65, their use of health services shot upwards. So, it seemed that Medicare eligibility after turning 65 years was causing a large wasteful increase in health care expenditures, relative to what one would predict before turning 65 years of age.

Of course, the economists very soon realized out what was happening. Prior to turning 65, people who had no insurance, or had private insurance that required large out-of-pocket copayments and deductibles, would *choose* to wait for surgeries and treatments until they were eligible for Medicare. After 65 years, with Medicare paying for most of the services, they could now visit doctors and hospitals at much lower personal cost. This would be the cause of the spike in health care expenditures. It was not necessarily Medicare inefficiencies that made expenditures rise; it was just the understandable choices of individuals responding to expanded health insurance coverage.

To make a before-and-after comparison of being eligible for Medicare meaningful, the economists decided to ignore the data on elective health care services, and concentrate just on the types of expenditures that individuals have no choice about, such as involved with visits to hospital emergency rooms (ERs). An emergency is, by definition, unplanned. Moreover, turning 65 years of age is not something that one can choose to be either. Any large jumps in health care outcomes post 65 years, called "regression discontinuities" (RD), could now be judged to be caused by Medicare, since they would not have happened due to any other known reason, and certainly not because someone had aged between the brief interval just before, and just after, turning 65 years of age.

In the case of ER visits, it turned out that Medicare eligibility (by some people being 65 and older, and not being under 65 years) saved lives. The seven-day mortality reduction was about 0.8 to 1.0 percentage points. The economists conjectured that Medicare might affect other dimensions of health than emergency visits, and that these effects may persist over a longer period of time than the nine months that they observed. This opened up the question for us whether something as widespread as dementia might also be something that Medicare eligibility can mitigate. So, we used the RD strategy in our estimation of the effectiveness of Medicare eligibility in reducing dementia symptoms.

ESTIMATING THE THREE STEPS FOR THE BENEFITS OF MEDICARE ELIGIBILITY

For the benefits, we again use the three steps presented in the last chapter. Recall that the benefits formula was:

$$B = [Valuation] \text{ of } [Change \text{ } in \text{ } Quantity] \text{ from } [Change \text{ } in \text{ } Dementia]$$
from an intervention

Step 1

The change in dementia from Medicare eligibility (the intervention) was obtained from running a regression equation, with CDR-SB as the dependent variable on Medicare eligibility and a set of controls.[13] Since we saw in the last chapter that years of education was a significant independent variable determining dementia, education was now added to the list of controls. The set of controls that were found to be statistically significant (not obtained by chance) were:

- Male (not female).
- APOE gene e4 (1 and 2 copies).
- Sibling with dementia.
- Height.
- Education (in logarithmic form).

The only difference with this set of controls from those used in the last chapter (apart from now adding education as a control instead of being the intervention) is the inclusion of height, which is another hereditary factor determining dementia (a person's height is basically determined at birth if not stunted by malnutrition).

Following the logic of the RD causality strategy we explained earlier, which looks at dementia symptoms before and after Medicare eligibility, which is at age 65, a person's age is not included as a separate control variable, but is split into two parts, age before 65 and age after 65. Age – 65 is called the "assignment variable." The full regression equation's list of independent variables thus consisted of Medicare eligibility and Age – 65, together with the controls listed above.[14] The result of running this regression equation combination can be seen visually by looking at Figure 4.1.

Figure 4.1 maps the assignment variable on the horizontal axis against the dementia symptoms measure on the vertical axis. On the horizontal axis, Age – 65 = 0 at age 65. Thus, the assignment variable is negative to the left of 65 years and is positive after 65 years. Before the age of 65, the regression line has a rising slope, to reflect the fact that dementia rises with age. But, at the age of 65, something dramatic takes place, that is, the regression discontinuity occurs. The line shifts down by almost one point, meaning that the CDR-SB has fallen by 0.9.

This is what Medicare eligibility achieves. After the age of 65, dementia symptoms continue to rise, even though Medicare continues, with a regression line that has a steeper slope.[15] This is because dementia (inevitably at present) rises progressively with older age. However, this does not negate the fact that, for a while, dementia symptoms have actually been reduced by nearly one point because Medicare eligibility existed.

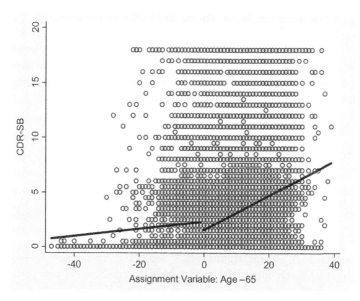

Figure 4.1   *Dementia symptoms rise with age, but at 65 years,*
when people are eligible for Medicare, symptoms
dramatically decline by nearly one point

Step 2

As to how changing dementia affects residential location, the mechanism is similar to that for the education intervention. The Change in Quantity is again going to be the change in dependent living from the change in dementia. The difference is that there now is an intermediate stage working through changes in the QoL as measured by the GDS. The dementia reduction increases a person's QoL by lowering the GDS. This in turn alters how much people switch to independent living. This is because both dementia and the dependent living conditions of a person affect a person's QoL. To see this clearly, we break up the relation between dementia and residence into two parts as follows:

$$\left[\frac{Change\ in\ Dependent\ Living}{Change\ in\ Dementia}\right] = \left[\frac{Change\ in\ QoL}{Change\ in\ Dementia}\right]\left/\left[\frac{Change\ in\ QoL}{Change\ in\ Dependent\ Living}\right]\right.$$

To estimate the two parts, a regression is run with the GDS as the dependent variable and CDR-SB and the levels of independent living as the main independent variables.[16] For the first part, a unit change in dementia reduced the QoL by –0.0416. The size of this reduction was the same for any type of residence a person was living in. For the second part, the QoL change depended on the extent of independent living. Recall from the last chapter that there were four levels of independent living corresponding to four different levels of caregiver costs:

1. Able to live independently.
2. Requires some assistance with complex activities.
3. Requires some assistance with basic activities.
4. Completely dependent.

We again focus on the three levels of dependent living (levels 2 to 4) as it is these outcomes that are lowered when independent living is increased by any dementia reduction.

- Level 2: A change from level 2 dependent living increased QoL by 0.4026. Dividing 0.0416 by 0.4026, to combine the two parts as explained in the equation above, produces a 0.1033 reduction in level 2 living from a one-unit reduction in dementia symptoms.
- Level 3: A change from level 3 dependent living increased QoL by 0.3464. Dividing 0.0416 by 0.3469 produces a 0.1200 reduction in level 3 living per unit reduction in dementia symptoms.
- Level 4: A change from level 4 dependent living increased QoL by 0.2165. Dividing 0.0416 by 0.2165 produces a 0.2165 reduction in level 4 living per unit reduction in dementia symptoms.

Step 3

As with the education intervention, the value of reducing dependent living is going to be measured by the caregiving cost savings that the change in residence generates. We will use the same monetary estimates as before. That is: there were assumed no caregiving costs associated with independent living; Level 2 costs were $23,188; Level 3 costs were $27,789, and Level 4 costs were the highest at $28,501.

Combining the Three Steps to Estimate the Benefits

Here we put the three steps together to estimate the benefits of Medicare eligibility from reducing the CDR-SB by almost one point. The results for the three steps, and their multiplication to form the benefits for each level of dependent living, are presented in Table 4.2.

We see from Table 4.2 that Medicare eligibility benefits are about $9,338 per person at the year of eligibility (it declines over time). Over half of this sum comes from the completely dependent living category, which is also the category of dependent living that is most affected by dementia being reduced.

Table 4.2   The total benefits of Medicare eligibility by residential level

Living Dependence		Step 1 Medicare Reduction in Dementia	Step 2 Dementia Reduction in Living Level	Step 3 Living Cost Savings per Living Level	Benefits Living Cost Savings
2.	Assistance with Complex Activities	0.9182	0.1033	$13,188	$1,251
3.	Assistance with Basic Activities	0.9182	0.1200	$27,789	$,3062
4.	Completely Dependent	0.9182	0.1920	$28,501	$5,025
Total Benefits					$9,338

Source: Table constructed by the author based on Brent (2018b), op. cit.

Estimating the Costs of Medicare Eligibility

We have just seen that the Medicare eligibility benefits were around $9,338 per person. To give some perspective on the size of these benefits, we can refer to the Medicare cost figures in a recent study. For 2010, the per capita Medicare annual cost per person was $10,904 if an individual aged 70+ did not have AD and it was $17,444 if the individual did have AD.[17] The difference in these two cost figures, which is $6,540, approximates the additional cost to Medicare if someone's dementia symptoms are not reduced.

Carrying out the Beginnings of a CBA of Medicare Eligibility

Compared to this cost of $6,540, the estimated $9,338 benefits of initial Medicare eligibility lowering dementia symptoms are relatively large. The estimated dementia benefits of Medicare eligibility on their own outweigh the costs by $2,798 per person, at least for the first few years after eligibility. Moreover, Medicare eligibility has many other types of health care benefits, as exemplified by the mortality reductions found related to ERs that we referred to earlier in this chapter. These mortality monetary benefits of Medicare need to be added to the caregiving cost savings we have estimated.[18]

In addition, it is an oversimplification to assume that with independent living there are no caregiver costs, and therefore no benefits to be had, for this residential level when dementia is reduced from an intervention. Caregiving costs may be reduced for family members, but dementia still requires some social support services even when older adults dwell in independent living. For example, take the case of adult day service centers: 30 percent of individuals using adult day service centers have dementia. Overall, 69 percent of adult day service programs offer specific programs for individuals with dementia, and 14 percent of adult day service centers primarily serve individuals with dementia.[19] The caregiver costs of these services would also be saved when dementia symptoms are reduced making the net-benefits of Medicare eligibility even larger.

RELEVANCE OF THE MEDICARE ELIGIBILITY RESULTS FOR LMICS

We have just seen that in the USA, by older adults being eligible for Medicare, and thereby having greater access to health services, dementia symptoms have been reduced and the benefits exceed the costs. This finding is especially relevant to LMICs because, at present, most of them do not have public health insurance for older adults, and private health insurance does not provide well for those with dementia, as we now see.

A recent large study examined the access of older adults (65 years and older) to health insurance and services in nine LMICs: urban and rural sites in China, India, Mexico, and Peru; urban sites in Cuba, Dominican Republic, Puerto Rico, and Venezuela; and a rural site in Nigeria.[20] These were the main findings:

- The proportion using health care services from all the main sources (government primary care, hospital outpatient, private doctor, traditional healer, and other community medical services) ranged among sites from 6 percent (rural China) to 82 percent (Puerto Rico).
- Health care services usage was greater for those with a larger number of physical impairments and depressive episodes, and who had higher education and were provided with health insurance. Usage was consistently lower across sites for those with a dementia diagnosis (either by the 10/66 criteria or DSM-IV criteria, or both).

People with dementia cannot receive services if health care service access is not available as in many LMICs. But also important is that what access that does exist carries with it special support for the special needs of those with dementia. The study pointed out that people with dementia may not be good at seeking help for their special needs. Having a system like Medicare would probably increase access and reduce barriers to care for those with dementia.

The study concluded that the variation in health care service use across sites could be explained by the extent of out-of-pocket expenses and the ability of older adults to afford them.

The importance of reducing out-of-pocket expenses can be seen in the case of Ghana. Although across SSA, only a small number of health insurance schemes have attained 30 percent coverage of their populations, and that mean coverage barely exceeds 10 percent, around 66 percent of Ghanaians are enrolled in a national health scheme. Membership requires payment of an annual registration fee, ranging from \$10 to \$30, according to the socio-economic profile of the registration district. People over the age of 69 years are exempt from the registration fee. This helps to explain why rates of enrollment are higher at 63 percent for those aged over 70, relative to 32 percent for adults aged 18 to 49.[21] However, even in Ghana, having health insurance did not ensure that the poor older adults in rural areas received increased health care utilization.[22]

SUMMARY AND CONCLUSIONS

In this chapter, we examined Medicare eligibility as the second CBA in the set of new interventions for reducing dementia symptoms. We followed the same three-step framework for estimating benefits. Just as with the education CBA, the quantity that was used to value the reduction in dementia symptoms brought about by Medicare eligibility was defined by increases in independent living, which in turn generated caregiver cost savings. The difference this time was that there was an intermediate stage linking the increase in independent living and the reduction in dementia symptoms. First, the reduction in dementia symptoms increased the QoL of a person. Then this QoL improvement translated into more people willing to go into independent living. Thus, the more a person's QoL was increased from reducing dementia symptoms, the more people transferred to independent living, and the greater were the caregiver cost savings.

Controlling for all of the usual determinants of dementia symptoms, such as age, gender, and hereditary factors, and also including years of education, it was estimated that being eligible for Medicare reduced the CDR-SB by 0.9182, nearly a one-point improvement. As we explained in Chapter 2, a 0.5-point drop in the CDR-SB should be interpreted to be a meaningful improvement. Recall that CDR-SB = 0.5 means that *some* signs of dementia are present. So, a 0.5-point reduction from 0.5 to 0 signifies that now no signs of dementia are present. However, most of the time, the starting point for the CDR-SB will be much higher than 0.5. Therefore, a 0.5 reduction can still be meaningful, even though it will rarely indicate that *all* signs of dementia have been eliminated. Compared to 0.5, the 0.9182 reduction does signal that Medicare eligibility is clearly an effective intervention for dementia.

We can be confident that the 0.9182 estimated reduction in the CDR-SB is causal because of the regression discontinuity strategy we adopted. Dementia symptoms usually rise continuously with aging across all years. Yet at the age of 65, at the exact time of Medicare eligibility, dementia symptoms not only did not rise, but actually fell. The downward effect was not permanent, as subsequently, dementia symptoms continued to rise with age as expected. But this does not obviate the fact that an improvement did occur for a while.

We documented the type of services that were expanded for older adults with dementia due to Medicare eligibility. The added services included emergency hospital care, an Annual Wellness Visit, and expanded drug coverage. The precise mechanism by which these extra services provided led to the drop in dementia symptoms cannot be known for sure. However, we have discovered that the mechanism worked by increasing the QoL of those receiving the extra services. The strength of the increase in the QoL varied by the level of residential independence, ranging from 0.2146 to 0.4026 as the independence level increased. Consequently, the transfer to independent living varied from 0.1033 to 0.1920. The end result was that the benefits in terms of residential care cost saving ranged from $1,251 to $5,025 for a total of $9,338 per person eligible for Medicare. These benefits exceeded the $6,540 costs of the extra services that someone with dementia required under Medicare. Providing for Medicare eligibility was both effective and socially worthwhile.

The relevance of the Medicare eligibility intervention for LMICs is direct. Medicare is a public health insurance program. It provided extra health services for those with dementia and in this way reduced dementia symptoms. LMICs, on the whole, do not provide public health insurance. Private health insurance is patchy. When they do exist, private health insurance schemes often require large out-of-pocket expenditures that limit access to poorer, older adults. Yes, as we noted earlier, Medicare does also, in some of the parts, require out-of-pocket expenditures. But this was not an insurmountable barrier to health care service access for those with dementia in the USA.

In this context, it is important to point out that older adults living in LMICs are more likely to be poor, as unlike in the USA, they have limited pension schemes; and when they exist, as in southern SSA, they rely more on contributory pensions for those in the formal sector rather than social pensions for all.[23] Many older adults in the USA have been taken out of poverty by having Social Security. At present, without the equivalent of Medicare, older adults with dementia in LMICs are receiving fewer health services than older adults without dementia and even younger healthier adults. We have learned that persons with dementia, because of the very nature of the disease itself, are often unable to articulate their health care needs to providers themselves. The fact that older adults with dementia in the USA do actually receive additional health care services under Medicare, and this reduces dementia symptoms, attests to the effectiveness and desirability of a Medicare equivalent program to be provided for this group in LMICs.

The contribution of this chapter to the analysis of the rest of the CBAs in this book is three-fold.

- First, because we have shown that Medicare eligibility is causally related to our CDR measure of dementia, it can be added (like years of education) to the list of controls for the equations estimating the effectiveness for the other dementia interventions.
- Second, by using the GDS as a measure of the QoL for persons with dementia in this chapter, we have an instrument available to use when we in the next chapter switch from using independent living savings to value benefits, to an outcome variable that is to be expressed in terms of people's QoL.
- Third, the economics literature on Medicare eligibility reminded us that greater access to health care services can save lives. Thus, using the saving of life years can be a further outcome measure to use to value benefits in CBAs of dementia. Although we did not need to include saving lives as a category of benefits to demonstrate the desirability of Medicare eligibility in this chapter, in Chapters 6 and 7, when we evaluate the corrective lenses and avoiding nursing homes interventions, saving life years will be the major outcome variable used to value the benefits in these CBAs.

NOTES

1. This chapter covers the CBA in Brent, R.J. (2018b), "Estimating the Monetary Benefits of Medicare Eligibility for Reducing the Symptoms of Dementia", *Applied Economics*, 50, 6327–6340.
2. Alzheimer's Disease International (2015), *World Alzheimer's Report 2015. The Global Impact of Dementia: An Analysis of Prevalence, Incidence, Costs and Trends*, page 53.
3. Sheikh, J.L. and Yesavage, J.A. (1986), "Geriatric Depression Scale: Recent Evidence and Development of a Shorter Version", *Clinical Gerontology*, 5, 165–173.
4. Medicare also covers people with certain disabilities or end-stage kidney failure. Everyone who turns 65 is eligible for Medicare if they receive Social Security cash benefits or currently reside in the USA, either as a US citizen

or a permanent US resident who has lived in the USA continuously for five years prior to applying.

5. Post hospitalizations, residents qualify for SNF care when changes in their conditions are likely and thus require skilled observation and assessment, or when they are prescribed complex services.

6. Although nursing homes are more commonly called skilled nursing facilities (SNFs), there is a distinction between them. NHs provide permanent custodial assistance, while SNFs are more often temporary.

7. LaMantia, M.A., Stump, T.E., Messina, F.C., Miller, D.K., and Callahan, C.M. (2016), "Emergency Department Use among Older Adults with Dementia", *Alzheimer Disease and Associated Disorders*, 30, 35–40.

8. Fowler, N.R., Chen, Y-F., Thurton, C.A., Men, A., Rodriguez, E.G., and Donohue, J.M. (2013), "The Impact of Medicare Prescription Drug Coverage on the Use of Antidementia Drugs", *BioMed Central Geriatrics*, 13, 37.

9. Any QoL measure for older adults with dementia faces numerous challenges; see Logsdon, R.G., Gibbons, L.E., McCurry, S.M., and Teri, L. (2002), "Assessing Quality of Life in Older Adults with Cognitive Impairment", *Psychosomatic Medicine*, 64, 510–519. People with dementia have varying deficits of memory, attention, judgment, insight, and communication that could limit their ability to respond to questions about their own subjective states. Depression, agitation, or psychosis may affect QoL ratings; and what determines QoL at the early stages of dementia (such as the preservation of intellectual capacity) may be different from the determinants at later stages (such as safety and comfort). Nonetheless, there are good reasons, explained in the text, why the total GDS is a suitable QoL measure for our data set.

10. Vagetti, G.C., Barbosa Filho, V.C., Moreira, N.B., De Oliveira, O., Mazzardo, O., de Campos, W. (2014), "Association between Physical Activity and Quality of Life in the Elderly: A Systematic Review, 2000–2012", *Revista Brasileira de Psiquiatria*, 36, 76–88.

11. See, for example, Graham, C. (2010), *Happiness around the World: The Paradox of Happy Peasants and Miserable Millionaires*, New York: Oxford University Press.

12. This whole section is based on two articles: Card, D., Dobkin, C., and Maestas, N. (2008), "The Impact of Nearly Universal Health Insurance Coverage on Health Care Utilization: Evidence from Medicare", *American Economic Review*, 98, 2242–2258; and Card, D., Dobkin, C., and Maestas, N. (2009), "Does Medicare Save Lives?" *Quarterly Journal of Economics*, 124, 597–636.

13. The full statistical specification of the Medicare on dementia symptoms regression in step 1 is equation (7) in Brent (2018b), op. cit., and all the estimation results are in Table 4. For step 2, the specification of the dementia symptoms on the GDS regression is equation (5); and the estimation results are in Table 3.

14. Strictly, the complete regression equation also had an interaction term for the Assignment Variable and Medicare eligibility to allow for the slope of the assignment variable to vary before and after the age of 65 years. So, the

estimation techniques became the varying slopes RD design. For the results of the changing slopes estimation, see the next note.

15. Figure 4.1 also confirms visually the fact that the slope of the assignment variable after the age 65 cut-off is much greater than the slope before the cut-off age. In Figure 4.1 the slope for the assignment variable before 65 years was only 0.0378, while the slope for the assignment variable after 65 years was almost four times greater at 0.1457. Figure 4.1 thus confirms that the varying slopes RD model is the more appropriate one as it allows the initial Medicare eligibility effect to decline over time.

16. Since the GDS dependent variable is simply an index of satisfaction, any independent variables included (and we use as controls a large number of health variables, such as drinking and smoking behavior) means that causality is not an issue with this part of the estimation of benefits.

17. Zissimopoulos, J., Crimmins, E., and St. Clair, P. (2015), "The Value of Delaying Alzheimer's Disease Onset", *Forum for Health Economics and Policy*, 18, 25–39.

18. How to value reductions in mortality is covered in detail in Chapter 6 with the vision correction CBA, and in Chapter 7 with the avoiding of nursing homes CBA.

19. Alzheimer's Disease International (2015), op. cit., page 53, gives many details of other extra caregiving costs that looking after people with dementia involves. For example, in the USA, caregivers of people with dementia were more likely than caregivers of people with other conditions to be required to provide help with getting in and out of bed (54 percent vs. 42 percent), dressing (40 percent vs. 31 percent), toileting (32 percent vs. 26 percent), bathing (31 percent vs. 23 percent), managing incontinence (31 percent vs. 16 percent), and feeding (31 percent vs. 14 percent). In the Dominican Republic and in China, among those needing care, those with dementia stood out as being more disabled, as needing more support with core activities of daily living, and as being more likely to have paid caregivers. Overall, dementia caregivers experienced more strain than caregivers of those with other health conditions.

20. Albanese, E., Liu, Z., Acosta, D., Guerra, M., Huang, Y., Jacob, K.S., et al. (2011), "Equity in the Delivery of Community Healthcare to Older People: Findings from 10/66 Dementia Research Group Cross-Sectional Surveys in Latin America, China, India and Nigeria", *BMC Health Services Research*, 11, 153.

21. Alzheimer's Disease International (2017), *Dementia in Sub-Saharan Africa: Challenges and Opportunities*, ADI, London, September 2017.

22. van der Wielen, N., Channon, A.C., and Falkingham, J. (2018), "Does Insurance Increase Healthcare Utilization among Rural-Dwelling Older Adults? Evidence from the National Health Insurance Scheme in Ghana", *BMJ Global Health*, 3: e000590.

23. Alzheimer's Disease International (2017), op. cit., page 54.

5. Hearing aids

Providing years of education and public health insurance are interventions that require a large investment of funds involving groups of individuals. We now consider the CBA of an intervention that is much less expensive and can be undertaken by individuals themselves without necessarily involving collective action. This intervention entails the purchase and use of a hearing aid (HA) for those with hearing loss (HL).[1]

For the years of education and Medicare eligibility CBAs, the outcome variable that was used in step 2 of the benefits formula was the savings in dependent living caregiving costs, which was obtained by people transferring to independent living because of the reduction in dementia symptoms from these interventions. For the Medicare eligibility CBA, the transfer to independent living was larger than for the years of education CBA, because we allowed for the fact that by lowering dementia symptoms, the QoL was increased. Since moving to independent living also increased the QoL, the transfer to independent living was made more worthwhile when dementia symptoms were reduced. However, the role of the QoL in this CBA was just an intermediary one. The final outcome was still to generate caregiving cost savings.

For the HAs CBA, we now focus on the QoL as part of the final outcome measure itself. HAs will be shown to decrease dementia symptoms, and this will increase the QoL, which will have a monetary value placed on it. This monetary value will be based on the value of a statistical life (VSL) literature, which is often used in economics to value changes in the quantity and quality of life for policy interventions, especially for regulations in the USA.[2]

CHAPTER OUTLINE

We begin with the background to HAs, in terms of reporting the prevalence of HL in older adults and explaining the relationship between HL and dementia. Then we describe our estimation strategy for establishing causality in the case of HAs. This is followed by the section identifying three hearing variables. Since HAs can produce benefits to wearers independently of reducing dementia symptoms, because it increases people's QoL directly, in this chapter we will provide estimates of the *total* benefits of HAs, being the sum of the direct effect and the indirect effect of HA's lowering dementia, and in this way also increasing the QoL. After explaining how the Geriatric Depression Scale (GDS) needs to be rescaled in order that it can be used as a QoL measure relating to the quality of an adjusted life year (QALY), we go through the three steps necessary to estimate the benefits of HAs. Once the benefits have been estimated, the CBA of HAs can then proceed. Showing the relevance of investing in HAs in LMICs is covered next and we close with the summary and conclusions section.

HEARING LOSS IN OLDER ADULTS AND DEMENTIA

According to the World Health Organization (WHO, 2017), an estimated 360 million people around the world have HL.[3] HL rises with age. In the USA, 18 percent of adults aged 45–64, 30 percent of adults aged 65–74, and 47 percent of adults 75 years and older report HL.[4] We know that dementia also increases with age (one-fifth of the US population have some form of cognitive loss by the age of 70 years).[5] Therefore, there is bound to be a strong association between HL and dementia.

There is such a strong link between HL and aging that the medical profession has a special term for age-related HL. It is called presbycusis. This HL is caused by the natural aging of the auditory system. It occurs gradually and initially affects the ability to hear higher pitched (higher frequency) sounds. Although it is progressive and irreversible, HL can be partially, and sometimes fully, offset by HAs. It has been reported that two-thirds of adults 70 years or older have an HL that affects daily living.[6] Since we have emphasized that interfering with ADL is our behavioral definition of dementia, it is by HAs allowing ADL to continue that we can say that HAs reduce dementia symptoms.

THE CAUSAL STRATEGY FOR HEARING AIDS

For the first two interventions, the NACC data set was used by examining clients at a particular point in time, that is, their circumstances at their first visit to an Alzheimer's Disease Center. Examining such data is called a cross-sectional analysis. This was appropriate in the context of interventions that did not change much over time. Years of education occur early in the life cycle, and Medicare eligibility occurs mainly in the later years, at the age of 65 years in the USA. For examining interventions that address client ADL needs that vary over time, the full data set can be employed that includes observations that record changes in symptoms and circumstances as people age. The full NACC data set covers individuals for up to 12 visits over a 13-year period. There were around 37,544 participants sampled between September 2005 and March 2017, with an average of 3.15 visits per client, producing 118,341 possible observations.

When data covers individuals over many different time periods it is called a panel data set. In the context of panel data sets, other ways of establishing causality are available, and we will explain here just the main method that is a "fixed effects" model. Recall that the main empirical problem for establishing the effectiveness of an intervention was that there may exist a third variable that could influence both the dementia symptoms and the intervention one is analysing. When this occurs, the relationship between dementia symptoms and the intervention could generate what is called a "spurious correlation." It is the third variable that could be causing the symptoms and interventions to move together, which may not have happened if the third variable had not existed and been changing. Thus, it was important to include in the estimation equation for effectiveness a large number of possible third variables that acted as controls in the estimation. The NACC data set was extensive, and so there were many controls used in the estimation of effectiveness for the two interventions covered earlier.

However, economists have pointed out that the possible third variable could be an "unobservable" which even a large data set does not fully allow for. Say that for any particular visit number at the ADC, the trained clinicians undertaking the interviews are the same persons, making the same clinical judgments. Then for those visits, clients are treated alike, and the subjective preferences of evaluators cannot be the main reason why one client's data is judged to be different from another's. Or, say, everyone's third visit took place in 2008, the year the "great recession" began. Then all clients had the same bad experience for visit 3. Including visit 3 in the estimation as a separate category would mean that the many-faceted, adverse experience of a recession was being controlled for across all clients. More generally, including all visit numbers as independent variables in the estimation equation is how the fixed effects strategy tries to establish causality in this panel data set.[7]

THE THREE HEARING VARIABLES

In the process of estimating the effectiveness of HAs to remedy HL, it is necessary to control for the fact that HL may not occur even without HAs, because some people have normal hearing from the outset. As a result, two cases of normal hearing will be identified: with and without HAs.

The benchmark for hearing loss that we will be using is the absence of functionally normal hearing. In an interview with the client, a clinician would assess HL if there were any functional impairment on the basis of there being a reduced ability to do everyday activities, such as listening to the radio or television, or talking with family or friends. We distinguish the two cases of normal hearing in order to test the extent to which the restorative power of HAs brings a subject up to a par with normal hearing. Our specifications of these two variables are:

- Hear 0 is designated as the dummy variable (1 or 0) for normal hearing without a hearing aid; and
- Hear A is the dummy variable (1 or 0) for normal hearing with a hearing aid.

Because HL is age-related, we must also control for the fact that normal hearing is expected to decrease with age. Thus, when we use the term "hearing variables" we are referring to the set of three variables: Hear 0, Hear A, and a client's age.

MEASURING THE QUALITY OF A LIFE YEAR

The GDS will again be used as the inverse measure of the QoL. Recall that Table 4.1 (in Chapter 4) lists the 15 ingredients of the GDS and each of these is scored such that the ingredient decreases the QoL. For the Medicare eligibility evaluation, where the GDS was an intermediary between the reduction in dementia and the level of independent living, the 15-point scale was not an issue. This was because whatever was the size of the GDS reduction, from the decrease in dementia symptoms from the intervention, the increase in independent living would increase according to the importance of the measured reduction. Now however, when the GDS is going to be the final outcome to measure changes in the QoL, the GDS units need to be adjusted. The QoL change is going to be used to measure how much *one* QALY is to be changed by a HA being used and, as we shall see, each and every QALY is then going to be priced (valued) separately. Clearly, one life year must have a quality on a scale of 0 to 1. One year cannot be worth more in quality terms than one year. Consequently, the 15-point GDS will be divided by 15 in order to be rescaled to have a maximum of 1 when it is to be used to measure a QALY.[8]

ESTIMATING THE THREE STEPS FOR THE BENEFITS OF HEARING AIDS

The three steps are contained in the benefits formula established in previous chapters:

$$B = [\textit{Valuation}] \text{ of } [\textit{Change in Quantity}] \text{ from } [\textit{Change in Dementia}]$$
$$\text{from an intervention}$$

Step 1

The effect on dementia from the HA intervention was obtained from a regression with CDR-SB as the dependent variable and the three hearing variables as the main independent variables. The statistically significant set of controls were basically the same as for the previous interventions, except that we now have a set of additional constant terms (intercepts) for each visit number, in order to implement the fixed effects strategy.[9]

Normal hearing without HAs (Hear O) lowered dementia symptoms by about one-third of a point (0.36), while normal hearing with HAs (Hear A) decreased symptoms by twice as much, 0.73 points. It seems that once a person has had normal hearing, and then loses it, having normal hearing restored by HAs is more effective for reducing dementia than having normal hearing without ever having experienced HL. Although a person's age cannot be altered by an intervention, it is interesting to know that each year of aging adds 0.03 points to a person's dementia symptoms.

Step 2

For the HA evaluation, the change in output that is going to produce value, from the decline in dementia symptoms, is going to be a QALY, which is the rescaled GDS unit. The GDS will be the dependent variable in a second regression equation with the hearing variables again being the independent variables.[10] Since we already know (from Chapter 4) that dementia lowers a person's QoL, dementia (the CDR-SB) was also included in this regression as a control with the hearing variables. The other controls were the same as for the regression in step 1 (again with the set of visit numbers as additional intercepts). The result was that: HAs (Hear A) increased QALYs by 0.0272 of a point; Hear 0 increased QALYs by 0.0036 of a point; a year of aging decreased QALYs by 0.0003; and reducing dementia symptoms increased QALYs by 0.0031 of a point.

The hearing variable that we are most interested in (because it is something that we can alter by an intervention) is the ability to obtain normal hearing by wearing an HA, that is, variable Hear A; although it may be interesting in itself to know that normal hearing without an HA (Hear 0) only had a small increase in QALYs. As we have just seen, Hear A increased the QoL (lowered the GDS) resulting in an increase in a QALY by 0.0272 points. This will be called the "direct effect" of HAs. In addition, there is an "indirect effect" of HAs, because HAs reduced dementia symptoms, and reducing dementia also raises QALYs. From step 1, we know that HAs reduced dementia by 0.73 points, and from step 2, we learned that reducing dementia by 1 point raised QALYs by 0.0031 of a point. Thus, the indirect effect of HAs was to raise QALYs by a further 0.0023 points (0.0031 times 0.73).

Step 3

With a QALY as the outcome measure, monetizing the outcome of HAs requires putting a price (social valuation) on a QALY. For this purpose, we will turn to the literature on the value of a statistical life, VSL, referred to in the introduction to this chapter. We will have a lot more to say about the conceptual base for this valuation in the next chapter, when the VSL will be the outcome variable for the intervention, and not a QALY, which is the case in this chapter. On the whole, the VSL is obtained from an individual's working experience, involved with trading off the greater risk of dying with some occupations (such as going down a coal mine) for higher wages to compensate for the greater risk. The oldest working age cohort covered in a large national VSL study, allowing for both age and cohort effects, was 55 to 62 years. For this cohort, the VSL for an adult aged 62 years was $5.09 million (in 2000 prices).[11]

This VSL estimate relates to a lifetime valuation for someone 62 years of age. To value one year contributing to a QALY, one needs to convert the lifetime VSL amount to the value of a statistical life year, VSLY. For someone with a life expectancy of 23 years, with a discount rate of 3 percent (as in the education CBA), and the quality of a life year of an older person being 0.7, the $5.09 million VSL amount results in a VSLY estimate of $442,857. Each QALY produced by the HA intervention will be valued using this figure.[12]

ESTIMATING THE BENEFITS OF HEARING AIDS

Here we present the direct benefits, the indirect benefits, and the total benefits of HAs.

- Direct Benefits: HAs directly increase the quality of a life year by 0.0272. Over 23 years, this is a lifetime change of $0.0272 \times 23 = 0.625$ years. With $442,857 as the value per life year, the direct benefits are $276,916 if HAs are fully effective (which is 86.28 percent of the time) so become $238,917 when adjusted for effectiveness.
- Indirect Benefits: By reducing dementia symptoms, which in turn increases the QoL, the indirect effect is to increase the quality of a life year by 0.0023 life years. With 11 years of life expectancy for a person with dementia (a person with dementia does not get 23 years), the indirect benefits are $11,021 if fully effective. With the 86.28 percent effectiveness adjustment, the indirect benefits become $9,508.
- Total Benefits: This is the sum of the direct benefits and indirect benefits. This makes the lifetime total benefits of purchasing and wearing HAs $248,425.

THE CBA OF HEARING AIDS

We have just presented the benefits of HAs. For the CBA to proceed, we also need to provide estimates of the costs in order that the net-benefits can be determined.

Costs of HAs

For the cost estimates we will refer to the literature which in the evaluation split the costs of HAs into two parts: the costs of the HAs themselves; and the costs of the post-fitting support services required to ensure that the HAs operate effectively, that is, restore the hearing so that it becomes normal again. The total costs per HA person were taken to be $1,119.[13] The data were collected for the years 1999–2001, so we shall assume that the cost estimates were in 2000 prices, which makes them comparable to the benefit estimates we provided earlier.

Most persons with HL (77 percent) experience the loss in both ears and so require two devices.[14] We will therefore double the $1,119 price to obtain a $2,238 estimate of the one-time costs of wearing HAs. The average length of life of HAs was found to be four to six years.[15] This means that for the 23 years of life expectancy that we were projecting for the direct benefits, people with HL would require around five pairs of HAs, making the lifetime costs $11,190. Discounting this sum at the usual 3 percent discount rate to the year 2000 would make the present value of the lifetime HA costs $8,498.[16]

NET-BENEFITS OF HEARING AIDS

Subtracting the lifetime costs of $8,498 from the lifetime benefits of $248,425 produce net-benefits (total benefits minus costs) of $239,927. This implies that for each dollar of costs for HAs, there are over $29 of benefits (as the benefit–cost ratio was 29.23). This makes HAs the most worthwhile of all the interventions that we have been evaluating, though most of the benefits do not come from reducing dementia symptoms. Nonetheless, HAs would be worthwhile even if the indirect (dementia) benefits were the only category of benefits and HAs were viewed exclusively as a dementia intervention. The indirect benefits of $9,508 exceeded the costs of $8,498 by $1,010. For each dollar invested in HAs, the benefits were $1.12, stemming from the increased QoL generated by the reduction in dementia symptoms from the HAs.

RELEVANCE OF THE HEARING AIDS
EVALUATION FOR LMICS

Unfortunately, HL is a bigger problem in LMICs than in richer countries. Therefore, adopting an HL intervention is even more important for these countries. It is not just the number of HL cases that is significant. It is the consequences of these numbers given the social and economic environment of these countries.

After adjusting for differences in age structure, the prevalence of HL was highest in LMICs and lowest in high-income countries. Age-standardized HL for persons aged 15 years or older ranged from 4.9

percent in high-income countries to 15.7 percent in SSA. It was highest at 17.0 percent in South Asian countries. Incidentally, globally, HL was greater for males at 12.2 percent than for females at 9.8 percent.[17]

As for age and HL in LMICs, nearly 63 percent of the population aged 60 and older with HL reside in these countries. Despite the fact that this older population makes up a small proportion of the population in SSA, the absolute number of older adults is growing more rapidly than elsewhere. The number of people aged 60 or over in SSA will double from 34 million in 2005 to 67 million in 2030.[18] HL will be even more of a problem in LMICs in the future.

The outcome variable used to value the CBA of HAs in this chapter was based on the QoL part of a QALY. The inverse counterpart of a QALY that is most often adopted in the literature for LMICs is a Disability Adjusted Life Year (DALY).[19] Instead of the quality of a life year, as in a QALY, a DALY uses the disability of a life year, which is also measured on the interval 0 to 1. Thus, to apply the benefit valuation method of HAs that we have just explained, it is the disability of a life year that is most relevant.[20]

To value a QALY we used the VSL approach to put a price on this outcome. In principle, the VSL approach could also be used to price a DALY. But, because the evidence on the VSL in LMICs is sparse, the WHO's (2017) estimate of the benefits of HAs for LMICs relied on pricing DALYs by the national income (Gross Domestic Product) of the country. Using this valuation approach, the global benefit of remedying HL was estimated to be $573 billion. Even on the basis of this very conservative benefit evaluation methodology (because richer countries obviously have higher national incomes than LMICs), high-income countries did not have the majority of the estimated benefits, as their share was 47 percent, leaving the LMICs' share as 53 percent.[21] Clearly, there is large potential for HAs to be found to be socially worthwhile in LMICs.

However, most of this benefit potential has not been realized to date. The WHO estimates that between 5 and 15 percent of people with HL in LMICs have received assistance, and even fewer are expected to have HAs, with less than 3 percent of HA-need being met.[22]

SUMMARY AND CONCLUSIONS

In this chapter, we examined the CBA of HAs. These HAs were shown to decrease dementia symptoms and thereby generate positive net-benefits on this count alone. These were called the indirect benefits of HAs, as the main reason why people purchase HAs was not to achieve these dementia benefits, especially as the existence of these benefits are not well known. Allowing also for the other benefits that come from HAs, which were called the direct benefits, produced benefits of over $29 for every $1 of costs invested in HAs. Therefore, in total, the benefit–cost ratio was 30 to 1. Clearly HAs were shown to be very socially worthwhile. The reason why the total benefits were included was that, in order to reliably estimate how much HAs lower dementia, and thereby increase the QoL, we also had to control for the fact that HAs separately also increase the QoL simultaneously with the dementia reduction effect on the QoL.

To estimate the benefits, we used a QALY as the outcome measure. This was used instead of relying on the cost savings from avoiding dependent living, which was used for the CBAs presented in previous chapters for the other dementia interventions. A QALY was chosen as the output for HAs because it is the most general outcome measure for any type of intervention, not just for health care, as any policy change one might consider must affect either the quantity or quality of a person's life.

It is the QoL (utility of a life year) part of a QALY that we focused on as the output measure in this chapter, and not the LY (life year) part, which was implicitly assumed to be unaffected. As before, we utilized the GDS as a negative proxy for measuring utility. We had to convert the GDS 15 instrument into the 0 to 1 interval scale to fit in with standard QoL measures.

To value (price) the QALYs produced by HAs, to form the benefits side of the economic evaluation, we used the relevant amount derived by the VSL literature. The underling conceptual base of the VSL is to find out how much people are willing to accept as wage compensation for a specified (small) additional risk of losing one's life in a particular occupation. To value the costs of HAs, we simply used the sum of the market prices for the number of HAs that a person with HL is likely to need to purchase over a person's lifetime.

HL has been shown to very prevalent in the USA. It is even more prevalent in LMICs. Thus, HAs are likely to be even more worthwhile for LMICs. To carry out CBAs of HAs in LMICs, QALYs can potentially also be used as the outcome measure using the methods explained in this chapter. The main difference is that for LMICs it is more relevant to use DALYs to replace QALYS. The WHO has already started evaluating HAs using DALYs, though their method for pricing QALYs is much too conservative, by relying on national income (GDP) estimates rather than individual preferences.

Once one uses DALYs as the outcome measure, one has an alternative way of quantifying the harm caused by HL. Based on DALYs, HL would affect 1.33 billion globally, much greater than the 360 million WHO estimate.[23] HL currently ranks as fifth on the global causes of years lived with disability. This is even higher than other chronic diseases such as dementia or diabetes. The number one cause of HL is aging, due to increased life expectancy. Other leading causes of the burden of HL are the widespread use of toxic-to-the-ear (ototoxic) treatments for diseases such as cancer and tuberculosis, and occupational and recreational noise exposure without appropriate ear protection.[24]

In the next chapter, when we report the CBA of glasses (vision correction), we will also refer to QALYs. However, this time, the focus will be more on the LY part of QALYs. As the VSL will again be used to carry out the CBA, albeit with a different emphasis, we will provide more of the details as to how the VSL is constructed.

NOTES

1. This chapter covers the CBA in Brent, R.J. (2019a), "A CBA of Hearing Aids, Including the Benefits of Reducing the Symptoms of Dementia", *Applied Economics*, 51, 3091–3103.

2. See, for example, Viscusi, W.K. (2018), *Pricing Lives: Guideposts for a Safer Society*, Princeton, NJ: Princeton University Press.

3. WHO (2017), *Global Costs of Unaddressed Hearing Loss and Cost-Effectiveness of Interventions: A WHO Report, 2017*, Geneva: World Health Organization. Licence: CC BY-NC-SA 3.0 IGO.

4. Donohue, A., Dubno, J.R., and Beck, L. (2010), "Accessible and Affordable Hearing Health Care for Adults with Mild to Moderate Hearing Loss", *Ear and Hearing*, 31, 2–6.

5. Fortunato, S., Forli, F., Guglielmi, V., De Corso, E., Paludetti, G., Berrentini, S. (2016), "A Review of New Insights on the Association between Hearing Loss and Cognitive Decline in Ageing", *Acta Otorhinolaryngologica Italica*, 36, 155–166.

6. Lin, F.R. and Albert, M. (2014), "Hearing Loss and Dementia – Who's Listening", *Aging and Mental Health*, 18, 671–673.

7. Strictly, including visits as controls is a *one-way* fixed effects model. Allowing for both visits and individual characteristics to be included as controls (additional constant terms) is a *two-way* fixed effects strategy. This two-way fixed effects model was used in the sensitivity analysis for the HA's CBA, and will be used to establish causality for the vision correction evaluation in the next chapter.

8. For a more formal explanation of the GDS rescaling process, see equation (1) of the HA CBA in Brent (2019a), op. cit.

9. The full statistical specification of HAs on dementia symptoms regression in step 1 is equation (6) in Brent (2018b), with the estimation results in Table 1. For step 2, the specification of the dementia symptoms in the GDS regression is equation (7) and the estimation results are in Table 2. The numbers in Table 2 were divided by 15 to produce the results in the text, because of the rescaling explained earlier. Brent, R.J. (2018b), "Estimating the Monetary Benefits of Medicare Eligibility for Reducing the Symptoms of Dementia", *Applied Economics*, 50, 6327–6340.

10. Note that in this second regression, GDS is simply an index of satisfaction. So, causality is not an issue. The regression shows how GDS is to be quantified, not what it is caused by. The GDS as measured cannot explain why HAs are, or are not, worn.

11. Aldy, J.E. and Viscusi, W.K. (2008), "Adjusting the Value of a Statistical Life for Age and Cohort Effects", *Review of Economics and Statistics*, 90, 573–581.

12. For a more detailed explanation of how the $442,857 price of a QALY was derived, see equations (9) and (10) of Brent (2019a), op. cit.

13. Abrams, H., Chisolm, T.H., and McArdle, R. (2002), "A Cost-Utility Analysis of Adult Group Audiologic Rehabilitation: Are the Benefits Worth the Costs?" *Journal of Rehabilitation Research and Development*, 39, 549–558.

14. Donohue, A., Dubno, J.R., and Beck, L. (2010), "Accessible and Affordable Hearing Health Care for Adults with Mild to Moderate Hearing Loss", *Ear and Hearing*, 31, 2–6.

15. This estimate also comes from ibid.

16. Note that the benefits were also discounted at the 3 percent rate and expressed in 2000 prices.

17. Stevens, G., Flaxman, S., Brunskill E., Mascarenhas, M., Mathers, C.B., and Finucane, M. (2013), "Global and Regional Hearing Impairment Prevalence: An Analysis of 42 Studies in 29 Countries", *European Journal of Public Health*, 23, 146–152.

18. Cohen, B. and Menkin, J., eds. (2006), *Aging in Sub-Saharan Africa: Recommendations for Furthering Research*, Panel on Policy Research and Data Needs to Meet the Challenge of Aging in Africa, National Research Council, page 57.

19. Murray, C.J. (1994), "Quantifying the Burden of Disease: The Technical Basis for Disability-Adjusted Life Years", *Bulletin of the World Health Organization*, 72, 429–445.

20. Although a life year (LY) is a part of both a QALY and a DALY, they are not measured in the same way. LYs in a QALY are the number of years gained from the intervention based on a person's life expectancy in the particular country; while the LYs in a DALY are the number of lost years from a disability that are averted from the intervention based on the maximum number of years of life expectancy by any country (which currently is Japan). There are a number of other differences between QALYs and DALYs, in terms of the different weighting and elicitation techniques employed, and these differences affect the relative outcomes in evaluations

of alternative interventions. See Robberstad, B. (2005), "QALYs vs DALYs vs LYs Gained: What Are the Differences, and What Difference Do They Make for Health Care Priority Setting?" *Norsk Epidemiologi*, 15, 183–191.

21. WHO (2017), op. cit., page 22.
22. Bright, T., Wallace, S., and Kuper, H. (2018), "A Systematic Review of Access to Rehabilitation for People with Disabilities in Low- and Middle-Income Countries", *International Journal of Environmental Research and Public Health*, 15(2165), page 2 of 34.
23. Vos, T., Allen, C., Arora, M., Barber, R.M., Bhutta, Z.A., Brown, A., et al. (2016), "Global, Regional, and National Incidence, Prevalence, and Years Lived with Disability for 310 Diseases and Injuries. A Systematic Analysis for the Global Burden of Disease Study 2015", *Lancet*, 388, 1545–1602.
24. Louw, C., Swanepoel, D-W., Eikelboom, R.H., and Hugo, J. (2018), "Prevalence of Hearing Loss at Primary Health Care Clinics in South Africa", *African Health Sciences*, 18, 313–320.

6. Vision correction

In this chapter, we cover the CBA of vision correction (VC).[1] At the time the evaluation was carried out, VC mainly involved the use of glasses. More recently, VC includes laser surgery. However, the estimates of the benefits of glasses can be assumed to carry over to any type of vision improvement. VC is like HAs, in that it is a dementia intervention that can be undertaken at the individual level, without necessarily involving the government organizing the production of the activity. Though, like HAs, individuals may need financial assistance with paying for VC.

The outcome variable for the VC evaluation will be related to the number of deaths that are averted by the intervention, in the form of the life years (LYs) that are saved. Older adults with poor vision are more likely to have falls, and be involved with driving accidents that are fatal. To value this outcome, we will again use the value of an LY that was obtained from the VSL literature that was employed for the HA evaluation.

In our analysis of vision impairment (VI), we will be dealing with the moderate to severe cases and not those who have become blind, which totaled 32.4 million in 2010; 76 percent of the 191 million people worldwide who have moderate to serious VI had a preventable or treatable cause. For these people, the VC intervention is the most relevant (covering 53 percent of the total). Apart from not having VC, the other main causes of treatable VI is having cataracts (18 percent of the total) and macular degeneration (3 percent of the total).[2] Normal vision is judged according to whether someone can read rows of letters of declining sizes in a chart 20 feet away; 20/20 vision is the outcome when one can read the eighth row of the chart.

CHAPTER OUTLINE

We start with distinguishing the two main types of VI and report how widespread is VI. How dementia and VI is related is then explained. The estimation strategy for establishing causality for VC that is presented will be the same as was used for HAs. What is different for VC is the outcome variable, which is going to be the gain in life years (LYs) part of a QALY, and not the QoL part that was used for HAs. Since the price of a QALY will again be derived from the VSL literature, we will explain in more detail the conceptual underpinnings of the VSL. The specifications of the VC variable, and the life years determinant, which is the reduction in mortality, are then explained. This is followed by going through the three-step procedure for estimating the benefits of VC in order that the CBA can take place. As with the HA intervention, VC will have a direct benefit effect, by VC saving lives for every older adult, and it will also have an indirect benefit effect, due to VC first reducing dementia symptoms and through this reduction, saving lives.

VISION IMPAIRMENT IN OLDER ADULTS

There are two categories of VI: short-sightedness (called myopia), where the eyeball is larger than normal, causing it to be naturally focused up close and people have difficulty in reading fine print; and farsightedness (hyperopia), where the eyeball is smaller than normal, causing its natural focus to be way out in the distance.

Even if one never had myopia to start with, when one ages, the lens of the eye hardens and loses its elasticity, meaning that it can no longer change shape to accommodate near vision. So one compensates for this by moving the object away. This is called presbyopia (age-related near vision) and the standard solution for this condition (until recently) is to buy reading glasses. Basically, myopia can be present in the early years (around the age of four years), and presbyopia appears in the later years (around the age of 45), when it affects almost everyone. Because, eventually, presbyopia affects nearly everyone, it is by far the most common cause of VI. Distance VI that is not corrected affects 123.7 million people globally, and the short-sighted VI from presbyopia that needed correction was over six times larger at 826 million.[3]

VISION IMPAIRMENT AND DEMENTIA

Given our behavioral definition of dementia, and our measurement instrument of dementia based on the CDR, it is apparent how VI can increase dementia and how corrective lenses (CLs) can reduce it. Orientation was one of the dimensions of the CDR. If one cannot see clearly, it is easy to get lost. Community affairs was another CDR dimension. It is difficult to have an independent function outside of the home without being able to see clearly. With VL, one is unable to accompany others to movies, and so on. The more isolated a person becomes, the more dementia will set in. Reducing isolation can also be thought to be one of the mechanisms by which HAs impact dementia symptoms.

THE CAUSAL STRATEGY FOR CORRECTIVE LENSES

We adopt the same fixed effects causal strategy for CLs that we used for HAs. This again involves taking advantage of the panel nature of our data set. When recurring visits are made to ADCs, various characteristics of those doing the dementia assessment, and those being assessed, are immutable. Even though some of these characteristics (such as personality traits) may be unobservable, the fact that they do not change reduces the chances that an unobserved third factor may be linking CLs and any reduction in dementia symptoms, helping to rule out spurious correlations. Also, having a large number of observed variables in our data set, which were used as controls in the regression equation used to estimate the effect of CLs on dementia symptoms, allows us to have some confidence that we have taken out from the error term many other third factors that could cause spurious correlations.

Conceptual Underpinnings of the VSL

The value of saving a person's life is often thought to be infinite. The drawback with this way of thinking is that it paralyses public policy decision-making. If saving one person's life is judged to be valued as having infinite worth, then using up all the world's resources to save that person's life would automatically pass a cost-benefit test and be approved. But, what about the rest of the world? Everybody else would have nothing to live on. Sacrificing billions of lives to save one person's life cannot be justified. This is even truer when one considers the possibility that some people's lives cannot be saved, even when all the world's resources are devoted to the task. Some people have incurable diseases that will kill them no matter what is done for them medically. At this time, one in ten people who contract the serious bacterial infection that causes meningococcal disease will die even when being treated, as the National Foundation for Infectious Diseases explains.[4]

The idea that the economist Thomas Schelling came up with to solve this valuation impasse was to switch from trying to value the saving of a life, to valuing a reduction in one's risk of death by a small amount.[5] This is the conceptual basis for the VSL approach. People make monetary gain/risk trade-off decisions every day, when they decide whether to cross the road in the high street where there is heavy traffic to shop at a store, or choose to go on an aeroplane as part of one's job.

The arithmetic is as follows. If someone is willing to accept employment with a $1,000 higher wage for a one-in-thousandth chance of dying on the job (say because you become a coalminer) then you are effectively valuing your life at $1 million. This is because one thousand times one-thousandth is equal to 1 and this is the full *probability* that you will die. So one thousand times $1,000 is equal to $1 million is the gain that you will get from accepting the unity probability of dying. This trade-off is called a statistical life valuation because it is the probability of dying that is being valued, not the certainty of dying. In this calculation, the probability is small and being scaled up to 1. It does not mean that the person would accept $1 million to sacrifice their life in its entirety (with certainty). What this means is that the greater the specified risk of dying, the greater the reward has to be. For example, doubling the risk to two-in-thousandth may require a ten-fold increase in the monetary gain that would be required as compensation (that is, $10,000), making the VSL amount $10 million and not $1 million for that particular risk.

Thus, when considering any VSL estimate one must be aware of the specified risk on which it was based. For the $5.09 million VSL amount that we have used in the last chapter, and will be using in this chapter, the risk of dying on the job is of the order of 1 in 20,000. Any intervention that one is evaluating must have a comparably small risk of dying in order to use the $5.09 million VSL figure. The simplest way of understanding the lifesaving part of the VSL concept is that if there is a 1 in 20,000 probability that someone will not die from an intervention, then if 20,000 people are benefiting from the intervention, it will mean that, on average, one person will not die as a gain from the intervention. The person whose life is saved is not known in advance.

Although the conceptual base for the VSL is clear, in practice there are many considerations that the literature has considered to be important in fixing a precise figure.[6] For example, does one use a work-related trade-off based on revealed preference behavior; or does one use a stated preference approach whereby a general population survey is carried out and individuals are asked to report how much they would be willing to accept for a specified hypothetical risk of dying. The $5.09 million VSL figure that we are using is based on work-related, revealed preference choices. This approach is the one most often used in the literature. It has the advantage that it avoids the problem that in practice what someone is *willing to accept* for an increased risk of dying has almost always been found to be higher (sometimes as much as seven times higher) than what someone is *willing to pay* to reduce the same risk of dying. People over their lifetime regularly change jobs, sometimes accepting more risk (usually when they are younger) and at other times paying to reduce risk (usually when they are older). So at any particular point in time, when one has data on work risk reward trade-offs, one is averaging the two risk groups and thereby canceling out the valuation differences.[7]

There is one other practical consideration covered in the VSL literature that is of particular relevance for this book focusing on dementia interventions. How one is to die may be important in making the lifesaving valuations, whether abruptly or spread out over time, and this often varies by disease. When a death is not sudden, as with many types of cancer, a person has time to plan for the death by, for example, making funeral arrangements and by reconciling long-lasting family disputes. When the time of death is unexpected, which is the context of the work-related trade-offs for the VSL valuation that we are adopting, these planning possibilities are not available. Although dementia deaths are drawn out (what Nancy Reagan calls the "long goodbye" related to her husband President Ronald Reagan's dementia death) when at the terminal stage where cognitive impairment is most serious, planning by the person suffering the dementia death is not possible due to cognitive weaknesses. In this way, dementia deaths are like accidental work-related deaths. Recent research confirms this conclusion. VSL estimates for usually slow-moving cancers were not much different from those for non-cancer-related diseases. More generally, VSL estimates covering illness-related diseases and accident-related deaths were similar. And most importantly for our analysis, there was not a difference in the VSL estimates whether they did or did not cover diseases that affected the brain (which is the case with dementia).[8]

The Vision Loss Variable

NAAC clinicians used a functional impairment criterion for assessing vision acuity and hence judging VL. The test was whether the client, who usually wears CLs, has an ability to do everyday activities, for instance reading or watching television. It is the inability to do ADLs such as these that constitutes dementia in all our evaluations of dementia intervention in this book. The specification for having CLs was a dummy variable (1 or 0) if the client, who usually wears CL, has functional normal vision when wearing the lenses. Thus:

- VC = 1 for having functionally normal vision wearing CLs; and
- VC = 0 if any functional impairment exists wearing CLs.

Note that, by definition, if wearing glasses does not allow a person to have functionally normal vision, they do not have VC.

Measuring Mortality

In our data set, a person is judged to have died if the person is known to be deceased. The person is classed not deceased if the person is not deceased, or is unknown to be deceased. So the probability of being dead (P) is also a dummy variable where: P =1 if the person is known to have deceased, and P = 0 otherwise.

ESTIMATING THE THREE STEPS FOR THE BENEFITS OF CORRECTIVE LENSES

The benefits formula is once more:

$$B = [Valuation] \text{ of } [Change \text{ in } Quantity] \text{ from } [Change \text{ in } Dementia]$$
$$\text{from an intervention}$$

Step 1

The estimate of the effect on dementia from the VC intervention came from a regression with dementia symptoms (CDR-SB) as the dependent variable and CL as the independent variable. The main control was the demographic variable age, and this was included with the constant terms for each visit number to implement the fixed effects estimation strategy.[9] The main difference for the CL regression equation for dementia symptoms, with the HA regression equation, was that for CLs each individual was treated as a control by including an intercept for each individual.[10] Note that although HAs was a significant control in the VC regression equation, as one would expect from the last chapter, it was not used for the main estimation for VC because most of the sample did not wear HAs, so including HAs reduced the sample size greatly (by 83 percent) and this reduces estimation efficiency. (However, the results with HA as a control were also recorded if one is interested to know this.)

CLs reduced dementia symptoms by 0.19 points and each year a person ages increased dementia by 0.03 points (as in the HA estimation equation). Although the 0.19 points reduction from VC was much smaller than the 0.73 points reduction from HAs, as we shall see, this reduction will still be very valuable because CLs save lives, and saving a statistical life is worth millions of dollars.

Step 2

For the CLs evaluation, the change in output that is going to produce value is going to be a life saved through the mortality reduction from the CLs, both directly and indirectly through reducing dementia symptoms. The second regression equation therefore has as the dependent variable the probability of being deceased (given by the dummy variable $P = 1$ if the person is known to have deceased and $P = 0$ otherwise) and has CLs and CDR-SB as the main independent variables.[11] The result was that CLs had a direct effect of reducing the chance of dying by 0.0038, and an indirect effect via a decrease in dementia symptoms reducing mortality by 0.0006.

Step 3

The mortality reduction from CLs will start to be valued by the VSL of $5.09 million. This valuation applies to the age at which someone typically dies, which in our sample was at the age of 79 years. However, the expenditure on CLs to achieve this full life span was much earlier, at the age of 65 years. To make the benefits on the same timeline as the costs, this 14-year difference for the valuation of benefits needed to be discounted. The social discount rate used for all the interventions covered in this book is 3 percent. $1 obtained 14 years in the future, discounted at 3 per cent, has a present value of $0.642. Multiplying the VSL of $5.09 million by 0.642 produces the baseline VSL of $3.27 million.

ESTIMATING THE BENEFITS OF CORRECTIVE LENSES

We now present the direct, indirect, and total benefits of CLs.

- Direct Benefits: CLs directly reduce the chance of dying by 0.0038. Multiplying this probability change by the $3.27 million VSL amount makes the direct benefits equal to $12,426 per person.
- Indirect Benefits: CLs indirectly reduce the chance of dying by 0.0006 (by reducing dementia symptoms, which in turn reduces the mortality rate). Multiplying this probability change by the $3.27 million VSL amount makes the indirect benefits equal to $1,823 per person.
- Total Benefits: The sum of the $12,426 direct benefits and the $1,823 indirect benefits of CLs over a person's lifetime is $14,249.

THE COSTS OF CORRECTIVE LENSES

A study pointed out that eyeglasses were the least expensive of the CL options in the year 2000 (a year contemporaneous with our VSL benefit estimate) as refractive surgery was not common at that time. It was estimated that an individual's cost of CLs using eyeglasses was $226.48 (the eyeglasses cost $180 and $46.48 was for the eye examination). It was assumed that eyeglasses needed to be replaced on average every four years.[12] We will use these per-eyeglasses costs and replacement rate, and apply them to the same timeline and discount rate that were used to calculate the benefits.

The typical client buys the first set of glasses at age 65. There is a 14-year span until death at 79, over which time the client will have bought four sets of eyeglasses at a total, undiscounted cost of $906. If the four purchases take place at ages 65, 69, 73, and 77, the present value of the costs over the 14 years is $765 when discounted at the 3 percent rate.

THE CBA OF CORRECTIVE LENSES

To calculate the net-benefits, one takes the total benefits and subtracts the total costs. The total benefits for corrective lenses are $14,249. Subtracting the costs of $765, we obtain a net-benefits amount of $13,484, with a benefit-cost ratio of 18.63. CLs are clearly socially worthwhile. Importantly, the indirect benefits alone exceed the costs, which comes from CLs decreasing dementia, and dementia reductions lowering the mortality rate. If the dementia benefits were the only source of benefits, the net-benefits would still be positive at $1,058 with a benefit-cost ratio of 2.4.

RELEVANCE OF THE CORRECTION LENSES EVALUATION FOR LMICS

Judged by the number of people affected in 2015, VI ranked third globally, just below HL which was covered in the last chapter (anaemia ranked highest with 2.36 billion infected).[13] Just like HL, VI adversely impacted LMICs much greater than in developing countries.[14] A very comprehensive evaluation of different strategies to combat VI in SSA and South East Asia (SEA) reported many interventions that were very cost-effective.[15] Since Cost-Effectiveness Analysis (CEA) can readily be converted to CBA, by using a price to value the outcome variable, when we present the results of the comprehensive study we will convert them to cost-benefit estimates in terms of the benefit-cost ratio, whereby a ratio greater than 1 indicates a socially worthwhile intervention (having positive net-benefits).[16]

The outcome variable for the study was a DALY, which we explained in the last chapter was an alternative, inverse, measure of a QALY that is most often used in the context of LMICs. As with the WHO evaluation for HAs, the price for the DALY was determined by the national income for the country. This time the national income that was specified related to the whole region doing the interventions, which was around $2,000 in international dollars (one international dollar buys the same quantity of health care resources in SSA and SEA as it does in the USA). The other difference for this study from the WHO HA evaluation was that they also considered a $6,000 national income as an alternative DALY price. We report the study results using both of these DALY prices.

The study defined the various alternative levels of an intervention to be a "strategy" to combat vision (and hearing) loss. The strategies were expressed as "screenings." Each screening was a combination of screening for uncorrected refractive error and the provision of spectacles for those who needed them. Therefore, the results are directly relevant to this chapter on CBAs of VC. Examples of the different levels of screening for VC involved:

- Varying the frequency of the screenings (say annually or every five or ten years).
- Varying the coverage of any frequency of screenings (say 50 percent or 80 percent).
- Varying whether the screenings were for adults or for children (or both).
- Varying the screenings for children according to whether they were for primary school children, secondary school children, or for all children.
- Varying the screenings for children by age, whether they be 8 years old or 13 years old (or both).

Table 6.1   *Benefit-cost ratios for vision correction and hearing aids in SSA*

Intervention		Cost per DALY	$2,000 Benefit-Cost Ratio	$6,000 Benefit-Cost Ratio
1.	CLs for all schoolchildren, 80% Coverage	$190	10.53	31.58
2.	CLs for all schoolchildren, 95% Coverage	$242	8.26	24.79
3.	CLs for all schoolchildren, 15% added to intervention 1's 80% Coverage	$521	3.84	11.52
4.	HAs for all children and adults, 50% Coverage	$735	2.72	8.16
5.	HAs for all children and adults, 80% Coverage, in combination with CLs	$747	2.68	8.03
6.	HAs for all children and adults, 30% added to intervention 4's 50% Coverage	$766	2.61	7.83

Source: Table constructed by the author based on information in Table 4 in Baltussen and Smith (2012), op. cit.

Just for VC there were 18 different levels of intervention (there were 21 for trachoma, 6 for cataract control, 36 for HL, with 87 in total). Table

6.1 presents the benefit-cost ratios that we constructed for just three of the VC interventions and three of the HA interventions for SSA.[17]

Clearly, CLs are socially worthwhile in SSA and not just in the USA, even with the $2,000 DALY price based on national income, which we explained in the last chapter was very conservative, as LMICs have much lower national incomes than developed countries. A price three times the national income is much more likely to be correct.[18]

Intervention 3 requires further explanation. Intervention 1 involves screening 80 percent of all schoolchildren and this has a very high benefit-cost ratio of 31.58. Intervention 2 replaces intervention 1 entirely, and starting from scratch, screens 95 percent of all schoolchildren. The benefit-cost ratio is also very high at 24.79. Intervention 3 says that if intervention 1 had already taken place, expanding coverage further by 15 percent points would lower the benefit-cost ratio to 11.52 – still very high, but not as high as undertaking a 95 percent screening program for schoolchildren from the outset, which is intervention 2.

Also presented in Table 6.1 are the benefit-cost ratios for HAs, again assuming that screening has taken place. The results confirm the conclusion of the previous chapter that providing HAs is very worthwhile in LMICs.

Although Table 6.1 reports results just for SSA, Baltussen and Smith (2012) do provide results for similar interventions in SEA.[19] The findings are comparable to those in SSA. For example, the counterpart to intervention 5 in Table 6.1 for SEA had a benefit-cost ratio of 6.96, as opposed to 8.03 in SSA. In both cases intervention 5 was very much higher than 1. These results are very important for policy purposes, as they reveal that CLs can be provided *together* with HAs to obtain highly socially worthwhile interventions in LMICs.

SUMMARY AND CONCLUSIONS

Presby is a Greek word for "old age." So presbyopia for VI is like presbycusis for HL, a condition that affects older adults and can lead to dementia. The process is similar to HL. VI leads to disorientation and with this problem, older adults cannot carry out their usual activities of daily living.

The consequence of VI that we have focused on, which is the outcome measure that needed to be valued to estimate the benefits of CLs, was the loss of life that having VI uncorrected causes. The loss of life came about in two different ways: by VI leading to higher mortality directly, and also indirectly, by first causing dementia symptoms to occur in terms of disorientation, say when driving a motor vehicle. This loss of life was valued at $3.27 million per life lost, derived from the VSL literature. Although the probability of losing one's life could (arguably) be considered relatively small from the VC intervention, it was because a life was valued in millions of dollars that the benefits were sizable. The direct benefits were equal to $12,426 per person and the indirect benefits were $1,823 per person. Since the lifetime cost of glasses were $765, VC was socially worthwhile just from the indirect, dementia symptoms reducing benefits.

It is important to emphasize that when economists try to value mortality outcomes they are not trying to "play God." They are not trying to value an actual life. Rather they are valuing a statistical life, which is the small probability of losing one's life. This is a valuation that people are willing to make every day when they decide to cross a congested road when shopping, or occasionally have to make when they decide what job risk is worth accepting to get a higher annual wage. Note that even having a "safe" sedentary office job carries a mortality risk from the lack of physical activity.

The results of the CBA of CLs in the USA reported in this chapter are likely to be very relevant to LMICs, as VI and dementia is more prevalent in these countries. Although there are as of now no CBAs of CLs in LMICs working through a reduction in dementia symptoms (that is, estimating the indirect benefits of CLs) we examined a very comprehensive study showing that the total benefits of CLs was as high in LMICs as in the USA. This makes it highly likely that the indirect benefits of CLs would also have a benefit-cost greater than 1, and so be socially worthwhile on this basis alone. This study's results also confirmed that HAs in LMICs also pass a cost-benefit test. In fact, one of the interventions in both SSA and SEA combined CLs and HAs, and showed that together they combined to produce a very socially worthwhile joint investment.

The results of the comprehensive study of evaluations of VI and HAs in LMICs, which we examined in this chapter, highlighted one of the central principles of public policy based on CBA. That is, when it comes to evaluating interventions, details matter. There is hardly any policy significance in claiming that education is likely to be a worthwhile investment in any country without first specifying what type of education is being proposed, and who the target group getting the education is going to be. Similarly, the extent to which VC (or HAs) is worth investing in varied greatly according to which population group was being tested, how often they were being tested, and the extent of the coverage for the designated population group. What this simply means is that when carrying out a CBA of any particular intervention for dementia, one has to ensure that the benefits and costs of the main alternatives to that intervention are also being estimated for comparison purposes.

Although we used the VSL concept to value a QALY both in this chapter on evaluating VC and in the last chapter on evaluating HAs, the emphasis was entirely different. In the HAs chapter the outcome being valued was the QoL part of a QALY, and in this chapter on VC the outcome being valued was the LY part of a QALY, when a QALY is the product of the two parts: QALY = QoL × LY. A more complete evaluation would include both parts. In the next chapter on estimating the benefits of not living in a nursing home, both parts of a QALY are used in the evaluation.

NOTES

1. This chapter covers the CBA in Brent, R.J. (2020), "A CBA of Corrective Lenses, Including the Benefits for Reducing the Symptoms of Dementia", *Applied Economics*, 52, 1–12.
2. Bourne, R.R.A., Stevens, G.A., White, R.A., Smith, J.L., Flaxman, S.R., Price, H., et al. (2013), "Causes of Vision Loss World-Wide, 1990–2010: A Systematic Analysis", *Lancet Global Health*, 1, e339–e349.
3. Fricke, T.R., Tahhan, N., Resnikoff, S., Papas, E., Burnett, A., Ho, S.M., et al. (2018), "Global Prevalence of Presbyopia and Vision Impairment from Uncorrected Presbyopia: Systematic Review, Meta-Analysis and Modelling", *American Academy of Ophthalmology*, 125, 1492–1499.
4. https://www.nfid.org/infedtious-diseases/meningoccal-disease (accessed December 16, 2021).
5. Schelling, T. (1968), "The Life You Save May Be Your Own", in Chase, S.B. Jr. (ed.), *Problems in Public Expenditure Analysis*, 127–162, Washington, DC., The Brookings Institution.
6. A comprehensive resource is Viscusi, W.K. (2018), *Pricing Lives: Guideposts for a Safer Society*, Princeton, NJ: Princeton University Press.
7. Kniesner, T.J., Viscusi, W.K., and Zilak, J.P. (2014), "Willingness to Accept Equals Willingness to Pay for Labor Market Estimates of the Value of a Statistical Life", *Journal of Risk and Uncertainty*, 48, 187–205.
8. Hammit, J.K. and Haninger, K. (2010), "Valuing Fatal Risks to Children and Adults: Effects of Disease, Latency, and Risk Aversion", *Journal of Risk and Uncertainty*, 40, 57–83; and Robinson, L.A. and Hammit, J.K. (2016), "Valuing Reductions in Fatal Illness Risks: Implications of Recent Research", *Health Economics*, 25, 1039–1052.
9. The full statistical specification of CL on dementia symptoms regression in step 1 is equation (6) in Brent (2020) op. cit., with the estimation results in Table 4. For step 2, the specification of the dementia symptoms in the

mortality regression is equation (7) and the estimation results are in Table 4. The 0.0006 indirect effect of CL on mortality is obtained by multiplying the effect of CL on dementia symptoms (0.019) by the effect of the dementia decline on mortality (0.003).

10. Including the set of individual coefficients means that the estimation technique used was a two-way fixed effects model. Note that with a two-way fixed effects model one cannot use as controls time invariant variables (such as race, gender, and years of education) as was used in the HAs regression based on a one-way fixed effects model.

11. Because the dependent variable was a dummy variable, the estimation technique had to be different from one with a continuous dependent variable. In our case, Logit was the estimation technique.

12. Vitale, S., Cotch, M.F., Sperduto, R., and L. Ellwein, L. (2006), "Costs of Refractive Correction of Distance Impairment in the United States, 1999–2002", *American Academy of Ophthalmology*, 113, 2163–2170.

13. Disease and Injury Incidence and Prevalence Collaborators (2015), "Global, Regional, and National Incidence, Prevalence, and Years Lived with Disability for 310 Diseases and Injuries, 1990–2015: A Systematic Analysis for the Global Burden of Disease Study GBD 2015", *Lancet*, 388, 1545–1602.

14. Fricke et al. (2018), op. cit.

15. Baltussen, R. and Smith, A. (2012), "Cost Effectiveness of Strategies to Combat Vision and Hearing Loss in Sub-Saharan Africa and South East Asia: Mathematical Modelling Study", *British Medical Journal*, 344, e615. doi: 10.1136.

16. Strictly, benefit-cost ratios may give different rankings from using the net-benefits criterion. In general, a benefit-cost ratio discriminates interventions with large capital costs. Nevertheless, a benefit-cost ratio is the appropriate decision-making criterion when there is an initial period capital constraint. See, for example, Brent, R.J. (1998), *Cost-Benefit Analysis for Developing Countries*, Cheltenham, UK and Northampton, MA, USA: Edward Elgar, Chapter 2.

17. The numbers in our Table 6.1 were constructed from the study's Table 4 as follows. Their Table 4 reported costs per DALY. The benefits of $2,000 and $6,000 were also per DALY. Thus, dividing the benefit sums with the costs in their table produced the benefit-cost estimates. For example, for intervention 1, the average cost was $190. Dividing this cost into the $6,000 benefit figure produces the 31.58 figure in our Table 6.1. For interventions 4 and 6, we used the incremental cost figures in the study's Table 4.

18. This three-fold national income recommendation is from Brent, R.J., ed. (2009), *Handbook on Research in Cost-Benefit Analysis*, Cheltenham, UK and Northampton, MA, USA: Edward Elgar, Chapter 1.

19. Baltussen and Smith (2012), op. cit., Table 4.

7.   Avoiding nursing homes

In this chapter, we (initially) consider living in a nursing home (NH) as a possible dementia intervention. The defining characteristic of a NH is going to be that it provides skilled nursing and long-term care for older adults that was not available when living at home. We have seen in Chapter 4 that Medicare facilitated the provision of additional health care services for those who were eligible. This led to a reduction in dementia symptoms that provided benefits that exceeded the costs. One may expect therefore that NHs would also provide positive benefits. In which case the research issue with NHs would seem to be to discover whether these benefits were of sufficient magnitude to offset the costs of NHs, which are well known to be very high.

However, it turns out that each one of the potential benefits of NHs are not only not large, they will be shown to be negative! This means that the very notion of a NH as a dementia intervention needs to be changed. The evaluation of the intervention is transformed into one of *avoiding* NHs and thereby estimating the benefits of *not* living in a NH. As we shall see, there will be four categories of benefits that can be identified and estimated. Two of these benefit categories specifically relate to persons having dementia and these are the ones that will be analysed in greater detail.

CHAPTER OUTLINE

All four of the benefit categories related to NH residence that we will be estimating will use a QALY as the outcome unit, where both the LY and QoL parts are utilized. As in earlier chapters, we will use the VSL literature to value each of the four QALY part outcomes to produce the four benefit categories.

Two loss of benefit categories are caused by a reduction in the QoL from residing in a NH. B1 is the direct loss of satisfaction that the NH environment generates, for example, from the loss of independence. B2 is the indirect loss of satisfaction derived from the NHs first increasing dementia symptoms and then the rise in dementia symptoms reducing the QoL, as it interferes with activities of daily living. In addition, there are two loss of benefit categories derived from the LY consequences of living in a NH. B3 is the direct reduction in life expectancy caused by living in a NH from the lack of essential care by, for example, not preventing bed sores. B4 is the indirect effect as a consequence of NHs increasing dementia symptoms that reduce life expectancy. First, NHs heighten dementia symptoms and this will, as we already know from the last chapter, lead to a reduction in life expectancy.

Logically, as every QALY part produces negative benefits, there is a separate fifth benefit category of avoiding NHs. This consists of the saving in costs that no longer have to be incurred to reside in the NHs. Although there is no information in the NACC data set that allows one to estimate these benefits ourselves, we will at the end of the chapter give some rough order of magnitude for this fifth category.

The chapter is structured as follows. First, there is an introduction to NHs in the USA, in terms of their main characteristics and who lives in them. Then we explain how the QALY effects for all four benefit categories were estimated. We start with the two QoL parts, the direct and indirect components, and proceed to the LY parts, direct and indirect. This is followed by the section putting values on the QALY effects to produce the four benefit estimates. Each of the four benefit estimates presented is per person. To put these estimates into a national perspective we transform these per person effects into an aggregate sum. Included in this aggregate sum will be the addition of the fifth benefit category derived from the cost savings generated by avoiding NHs. We close with the sections examining the relevance of our findings for LMICs and presenting the summary and conclusions.

NURSING HOMES IN THE USA

The two main characteristics of NHs are who pays for them, and who owns them. Medicaid, government health insurance for those with low incomes and assets administered by the states, pays for 62 percent of the residents. Medicare pays for 14 percent of the residents, and only 24 percent of the residents pay the private rates set by the NHs themselves. The payment sources between Medicare and Medicaid vary over the length of the stay, because Medicare has day limits and Medicaid has income and asset limits. For example, in Pennsylvania, 52 percent of residents are at the time of admission covered by Medicare. However, by the end of their stay, only 10 percent of the residents are covered by

Medicare. In terms of ownership, 46 percent of NHs are for-profits, 48 percent are private and not-for-profit, and 6 percent are public.[1]

The typical resident of NHs is female (66.67 percent), white (79.31 percent), and is long stay (68.56 percent); 84.68 percent of residents were admitted from the hospital; the average age is 79.71 years. The NH population is particularly vulnerable. Mental health is an issue as 45.27 percent have dementia and 48.74 percent take antidepressant medications; 91.82 percent need assistance with dressing and 96.46 percent need assistance with bathing.[2] Because of the vulnerabilities of NH residents, it is very important to control for the lower health states of residents relative to non-residents. Of all the many controls that will be utilized in our estimations, as always, dementia will be the main focus of the analysis.

It is not just the levels of health states that will determine our NH and non-NH comparisons. This is because it is *changes* in the levels of the controls that we are able to detect by our use of panel data that vary over time. Thus, it may well be the case that many older persons with dementia enter NHs. But many older persons with dementia do not live in NHs. It is this comparison group, and their changing characteristics over time, that is relevant to knowing whether QALYs have changed more over time in NHs than outside NHs.

MEASURING THE QoL EFFECTS OF RESIDING IN A NURSING HOME[3]

To measure the QoL effects we will use the GDS index as we did for the Medicare and HAs evaluations. The GDS is a negative measure of utility that has 15 ingredients that was listed in Table 4.1 (in Chapter 4). We will, as with the HAs evaluation, rescale the GDS by diving by 15 to ensure that it is on a scale of 0 to 1 in order to apply to a single LY in the QALY measure.

The GDS is a particularly appropriate measure of the QoL of living in a NH because the measures in the literature on the QoL are much too partial and do not explicitly record satisfaction. Understandably, when the literature tries to measure QoL by inputs, it uses the number of skilled (registered) nurses, or the ratio of skilled nurses to residents, or having a minimum number of skilled nurses, since having continuous skilled nursing is the defining characteristic of a NH. Nonetheless, we need to know whether adding skilled nurses usually makes residents feel more satisfied with living in a NH.

Similarly, when the literature tries to measure QoL by outputs, such as the 179 deficiencies included in the data set collected by the Centers for Medicare and Medicaid Services (CMS), one needs to know how concerned the residents are about any particular deficiency. Even when the 179 deficiencies are aggregated by the CMS, to form a five-star rating award for any particular NH, what is missing is how much residents care about the ratings, not just those who are seeking to place a friend or relative in a NH. It is interesting to know that the five-star rating is inversely related to costs.[4] But, this still ignores the benefits side of the evaluation equation.

What makes the GDS a more useful index of the QoL of a NH is that it is the most comprehensive measure, as it reflects *anything* that can take place in a NH, even if that presence is as abstract as the "environment" of a NH. The literature has focused on the quality of care, when what is more important is the resident's *utility* of care, which is what the GDS measures. In this way, the GDS fits in well with one of the central normative principles of CBA. The principle is called "consumer sovereignty", which requires that the individual be the best judge of his or her own welfare.[5] Priority is given to the preferences of the persons most affected by an intervention, and not the assessments of third parties, no matter how well meaning those assessments may be for the residents.

ESTIMATING THE QoL EFFECTS OF A NURSING HOME

For the direct and indirect QoL parts of the QALY impact of NHs, we will refer to two regression equation results. One regression has the GDS as the dependent variable and NHs and dementia symptoms as the main independent variables. And the other regression has dementia symptoms (the CDR-SB) as the dependent variable and NHs as the main independent variable.[6] So we are effectively dealing here with steps 1 and 2 of our three-step evaluation framework for estimating benefits, which first tests whether the intervention (avoiding a NH) is effective in impacting dementia, and then sees the extent to which changing dementia affects an output of value (the QALYs).

The controls for the two regressions are basically the same. As explained earlier in this chapter, what is important is what changes when a person goes to a NH. Using our NACC data set in the form of panel data, as we did for the HAs and CLs interventions, allows causality to be established using a fixed effects estimation method. When a constant term for each visit number is included as a control, everyone with the same visit number has the same experience, whether the person went to a NH or not. Different visit numbers record changes in common experiences at a point in time by visitors to a NACC clinic (such as a recession) and in this way, "unobservables" are controlled for.[7]

This is also, for example, why we did not need to include race and gender explicitly as controls. A person's race and gender does not change from visit to visit and so cannot account for changes in the dependent variables. Age, on the other hand, does vary from visit to visit and must be controlled for as it affects all three of the main variables: NHs, dementia symptoms, and the QoL. Accompanying age as controls were health status variables (such as the heart rate and the Body Mass Index, BMI), all the other dementia interventions (Medicare eligibility, HAs, VC), and marital status (such as being a widow). Note that the years of education intervention was not included as a control variable precisely because it did not change in our sample from visit to visit.

From the dementia regression, we learn that NHs had a large impact on dementia symptoms because the CDR-SB increased by 3.2367 points on a scale of 0 to 18. This result is very important in its own right as it confirms that our labeling of avoiding living in a NH as a dementia intervention is indeed correct. It also sets the stage for the existence of an adverse indirect effect of NHs on the QoL, seeing that, as we shall now see, by NHs raising dementia, the QoL is reduced.

From the GDS regression, we find that a NH raises the GDS, and thus lowers the QoL, by 0.0217 points on a scale of 0 to 1. This means that for every year that an older adult resides in a NH, the QoL declines by 2.17 percent. As we shall see in the next section, the average duration in a NH is 6.4 years, which makes the QALY drop to be valued for B1 equal to 0.1388.

The GDS regression also revealed that dementia lowered the QoL by 0.0021 for every one point that dementia symptoms are raised. Since we know from the dementia regression that NHs increased dementia by 3.2367 points, we obtain a QoL reduction of 0.0068 (that is, 3.2367 times 0.0021) for each year of NH residency. For a 6.4-year duration, this results in a further 0.0435 QALY reduction from the indirect QoL effect that is needed to estimate B2. Although this indirect QALY effect may seem small, it is because one QALY is valued in millions of dollars that B2 will become a sizable amount.

ESTIMATING THE LY EFFECTS OF NURSING HOMES[8]

For the purpose of estimating the LYs lost by NHs, the NACC data set had to be reformulated so that survival analysis could be used for estimation. The reformulation involved augmenting the data by adding four time variables:

- The time of entry of an observation to the panel;
- The duration of an observation in the panel;
- The outcome at the end of the span (death or continuing to live); and
- Whether an observation was used or not (for some observations there were missing data).

The purpose of the four time variables was to convert calendar time into a time span from the time of entry to the time of death or censure (because future visits for those who did not die cannot be observed at the time the panel ends). In this way, life expectancy (in months) could be estimated for the duration of a person's life until death for those living in a NH and those not living in a nursing NH.

For the particular survival model chosen for estimation, which allowed one to control for health states and other variables before going into the NHs and, crucially, also after people have gone into the NHs, the dependent variable was the time till death, that is, life expectancy.[9] The independent variables were the chances of dying in and outside of NHs (the so-called hazard ratio which was a part of the estimation), the set of usual controls (age, gender, race, BMI, years of smoking, heart rate, Medicare eligibility, and years of education), and the visit number involved (to allow for fixed effects).

The estimated life expectancy results are shown in Table 7.1. Shown separately are the life expectancies for those living in NHs and those residing outside NHs, and the life expectancies for persons with four different stages of dementia symptoms. Recall that when we introduced the CDR instrument to measure dementia symptoms in Chapter 2, it was explained that the 0 to 18 scale could also be grouped into classes, to correspond somewhat with the official four-stage classification scheme used in the Alzheimer's Association's 2018 Report. The stages were: normal cognition, preclinical, mild cognitive impairment (MCI), and full dementia.[10] For the NH life expectancy study we are now considering, we basically use the same four-stage classification scheme that mirrors

Table 7.1   *Life expectancy with and without dementia in nursing*
                   homes (months)

Dementia Score	Life Expectancy in NH	Life Expectancy Not in NH	Difference
Stage 1	111	133	− 22
Stage 2	98	117	− 19
Stage 3	87	104	− 17
Stage 4	74	88	− 14
Weighted mean	77	118	− 41

Source: The table is an abbreviated version of Table 5 in Brent (2021a), op. cit.

the US prevalence rates in the 2018 Report. Stage 1 is no dementia with CDR-SB = 0. Stage 2 has the CDR-SB interval 0.5 to 3.5. Stage 3 has the interval 4.0 to 6.0; and for stage 4, serious dementia, the interval is 6.5 to 18. The reason why the CDR was grouped into classes was that it was thought unlikely that, by NHs changing dementia symptoms by just a decimal point or two, life years would be lost. Whereas with larger groupings, lives could be at risk.

On average, people lived 77 months (6.4 years) when living in a NH. This is the figure we used in the QoL part of the evaluation earlier in the chapter related to B1 and B2. Now we see that people lived 41 months (3.4 years) longer if they did not reside in a NH, controlling for many of the health state variables that generally determine life expectancy for older adults.

This fixes the loss from the direct LY effect at 3.4 years. With 0.87 being the average QoL of everyone in our sample, the loss of QALYs to be valued for B3 is 2.9580.

For those with stage 4 serious dementia not living in NHs, the life expectancy was 88 months. For those with stage 4 serious dementia symptoms living in NHs, the life expectancy was 74 months. The difference of 14 months is how much having serious dementia in NHs reduces one's life expectancy. We focus here just on the stage 4 serious dementia group, as they were 86 percent of those with serious dementia symptoms in NHs in our sample. The question now is how much of these 14 months is lowered by NHs raising dementia symptoms by 3.2367 CDR units. To be classified into the serious dementia group the CDR score had to between 6.5 and 18. We can therefore take the average score of 12.25 as being typical of those in stage 4, which means that the 3.2367 CDR units increase from living in a NH takes them 0.26 of the way to be classified as having serious dementia and losing the 14 months. The result then is that NHs cause residents with serious dementia to lose the equivalent of 3.64 months of their life expectancy, which is 0.3033 LYs. Again making the 0.86 QoL adjustment for these lost LYs, the QALYs to be valued for B4 is 0.2609.

THE FOUR BENEFITS ESTIMATES AND THE TOTAL LOSS

The third step for estimating benefits is to apply a monetary sum to the QALYs lost in the four benefit categories. As with HAs, the VSLY from the literature will be applied. For the NH evaluation, a QALY will be valued at $500,000.[11] The resulting estimates for the four benefit categories were:

B1. The direct QoL loss was 0.1388 QALYs times $500,000, which equals $69,400.

B2. The indirect QoL loss was 0.0435 QALYs times $500,000, which equals $21,750.

B3. The direct LY loss was 2.9850 QALYs times $500,000, which equals $1,479,000.

B4. The indirect LY loss was 0.2609 QALYs times $500,000, which equals $130,450.

Taken together, the loss from residing in a NH is $1.7 million per person. There are around 1.1 million people living in NHs in the USA.[12] This means that for the USA as a whole, the total loss of benefits amounts to $1.87 trillion.

As we pointed out earlier, given that there are no benefits and only losses from living in a NH, a fifth category of benefits of avoiding a NH comes into play, and that is the savings from not incurring the NH residential costs by not going to a NH in the first place. We can obtain a preliminary estimate of these cost savings by looking at how much Medicaid (which finances most of the NH expenses) saved from their policy of substituting home care for institutional care. A recent estimate was that 35.1 percent of the Medicaid budget was saved by this substitution.[13] Given that Medicaid NH expenditures totalled $170 billion in 2016,[14] the 35.1 percent reduction produces a sum of $59.67 billion. This makes the total loss from all five categories $1.93 trillion. To put this total loss into perspective, the gross national income of the USA in 2016 was $19.05 trillion. Thus, the loss of QALYs from living in NHs is worth around one-tenth of the entire total of goods and services bought and sold in the USA.

RELEVANCE OF THE NURSING HOME EVALUATION FOR LMICS

Palliative care is needed by 40 million people in the world, that is, care that reduces pain and suffering and not necessarily targeted to increasing life expectancy, so for this population, QoL is the focus; 69 percent of these people are those older than 60 years, and 78 percent of the 40 million live in LMICs. Therefore, the need for care of the elderly is large in LMICs. Despite this need, most elderly people in LMICs have limited access to palliative care, especially those in rural areas.[15]

The WHO point out that most of the long-term care that is provided in LMICs is carried out by families without any training or support. What organized, institutionalized long-term care that is provided in SSA is funded either by charities (faith-based and civil society) or private for-profit residential homes (for those able to afford them).[16] Thus, there is no overarching social health insurance undertakings like Medicaid and Medicare to finance long-term care in LMICs that takes place in the USA.

To appreciate the lack of financial public support in LMICs, and the reliance on out-of-pocket expenditures, consider the percentage of public expenditure on long-term care as a percentage of national income (GDP) in a selection of LMICs published by the International Labour Organization (ILO). As a benchmark for comparison purposes, note that it is 0.5 percent in the USA. The ILO found that the long-term care percentage was 0 percent in Mexico, Colombia, Chile, Brazil, Nigeria, Ghana, and Algeria. Even in India and China, whose economies have recently been growing the fastest of all the LMICs, the percentage is still only 0.1 percent.[17]

In the USA, long-term skilled nursing can take place outside NHs, but this is not a viable option for LMICs. In the USA, we showed that both parts of a QALY, the QoL and the number of LYs, could be enhanced by not living in a NH. This cannot be the case in LMICs, especially as there is a strong relationship between physical and mental health in all countries. Without palliative care (especially medicines), the QoL must suffer. Even with the traditional extended family in LMICs, mortality rates are higher for those with dementia and without social support.

For example, in Botswana, those in rural areas without social support (usually eat alone), have low physical health (are unable to rise from a chair without using their hands), and with cognitive impairment had significantly increased short-term risk of death. The estimated mortality rate of 11 percent was more than twice that among age-peers in several European countries.[18]

The WHO also emphasize that in SSA, few caregivers understand the nature of dementia and the ways it can influence behavior. Thus, caregivers are unsure about how to ease the burden and enhance the lives of those with dementia. As an example of the lack of dementia understanding, the WHO refer to accusations of witchcraft by older people's kin when they show a noticeable decline in their mental and physical capacities.

For an example of best practice for an intervention that was able to solve the lack of public financing for long-term care in LMICs, refer to the operations of Rand Aid, a non-profit-making organization in Johannesburg, South Africa.[19] There are two components of Rand Aid. First, there is the provision of a range of upscale retirement accommodation and long-term care for those who can afford it. Currently there are around 1,800 residing in Rand Aid properties, which includes 360 who live in long-term care facilities. Second, there is subsidized long-term care for 180 older people in need of 24-hour nursing care, which is financed from the income generated from those who pay for the accommodation (coming from the first component).

The retirement villages are sold on the life rights concept whereby residents buy the right to live in the villages until they die or leave. As Rand Aid always retains ownership of the properties, they can continue to sell the rights to subsequent residents after the termination of any one agreement. The cross-subsidization works by reimbursing 80 percent of the initial purchase price to the estate on the termination of the sale. This leaves a portion of the 20 percent to finance the accommodation and care of those who cannot afford it. It is important to note that the long-term care facility includes a specialized dementia unit. The demonstrated sustainability of the Rand Aid intervention can be confirmed by the fact that the project has existed for over 100 years (it was founded in 1903).

SUMMARY AND CONCLUSIONS

Although the justification for the very existence of NHs is that they can provide long-term care by skilled nurses on a 24-hour-a-day basis that cannot be provided at home, it is well known that NHs in the USA do a disservice for their residents. What is new about this chapter is that we provide quantitative monetary estimates of the extent to which the NHs provide this disservice.

In the process, we also provide evidence that NHs actually cause dementia symptoms to increase. In this way, we can justify the claim that the avoidance of living in a NH is a dementia intervention.

There were four benefit categories that emanated from our use of QALYs as the outcome measure for the evaluation of NHs. B1 and B2 were derived from the direct and indirect QoL effects of NHs; and B3 and B4 were based on the direct and indirect life expectancy effects of NHs. The total QALYs lost by residing in a NH was 3.4282 quality-adjusted years. The two indirect effects B2 and B4 existed only because NHs caused dementia symptoms to rise by 3.2367 points on a scale of 0 of 18, which is a significant increase. In total, the loss from these four benefit categories was $1.87 trillion. Since all four benefit categories resulted in losses, there was a fifth category of benefits, which involved the savings from Medicaid not having to pay for people to stay in a NH. This raised the aggregate loss of benefits to $1.93 trillion.

There exists an extensive literature by economists trying to explain why NHs produce such a loss of benefits in the USA. Examples of just some of the explanations include: the lack of competition (which enables NHs to reduce costs by reducing the quality of life of residents); government regulations (which specify minimum staffing levels, but may affect adversely those NHs above the minimum); and the lack of knowledge about the needs of their residents (in particular, related to appropriate pharmaceutical options and the need for physical activity). Any convincing explanation must include some reference to factors determining the absence of skilled nursing, since this is one of the main defining characteristics of a NH. In this regard, a recent study of the effects of raising Medicaid's daily rates is most relevant, as we now explain.

The majority of NHs in the USA are for-profit and the main source of the payments for the NHs is Medicaid. Given that Medicaid pays such low daily rates, especially relative to Medicare, NHs may try to cut costs in order to make a profit by hiring fewer skilled nurses. If one were to raise Medicaid rates, then more skilled nurses would be hired and NH outcomes would be much improved. It was found that the benefits (in terms of people's willingness to pay) for an additional nurse in Pennsylvania were $133,000 when the costs were $83,000, providing net benefits of $50,000 per nurse. Thus, more skilled nurses needed to be hired. To achieve this, it was estimated that a 10 percent increase in Medicaid reimbursement rates would raise the number of nurses by 8.7 percent, which translates to an additional ten minutes on average per day that a skilled nurse spends with a resident. This means that raising Medicaid rates would be an effective way of achieving a socially worthwhile intervention to improve NHs in the USA.

Even though the need for long-term care is greater in LMICs, public resources are not available to fund skilled nursing whether inside or outside of NHs. Private not-for-profit residencies would seem to be the way forward, with some element of cross-subsidization involved (to try to replicate the Medicaid model of providing long-term care for those with low incomes), which are bound to be those with dementia. Whatever support that existed for long-term care from families in LMICs in the past is likely to be diminished in the future, due to the weakening of the extended family support systems that is currently taking place. In SSA, this arises because of such factors as increased rural to urban migration, and the increased participation of women in the labor force who are the main caregivers of older adults.

Now that we have completed our explanations of the existence of five new dementia interventions, we can turn our attention in the last part of the book to the public policy implications of dementia interventions, starting with the link between dementia and elder abuse.

NOTES

1. Hackmann, M.B. (2019), "Incentivizing Better Quality of Care: The Role of Medicaid and Competition in the Nursing Home Industry", *American Economic Review*, 109, 1684–1716.
2. Fashaw, S.A, Thomas, K.S., McCreedy, E., and Mor, V. (2020), "30-Year Trends in Nursing Home Composition and Quality since the Passage of OBRA", *Journal of the American Medical Directors Association*, 21, 233–239. This paper reviews the QoL improvements in NHs since the Omnibus Reconciliation Act (OBRA) of 1987. Many regulations of NHs were instigated by this act, such as physical constraints on residents, which declined drastically over this period from 19 percent to 1 percent. Nonetheless, as this chapter shows, the QoL changes were not sufficient to achieve the result that NHs overall improve an older person's QoL.
3. The parts of this chapter that cover the QoL of NHs, and provide the final estimates for all benefit categories of NHs, is based on Brent, R.J. (2022), "The Benefits of Not Living in a Nursing Home", *Applied Economics*. doi: 10.1080/00036846.2021.1983141.
4. Dulal, R. (2017), "Cost Efficiency of Nursing Homes: Do Five-Star Quality Ratings Matter?" *Health Care Management Science*, 20, 316–325.

5. For a text on CBA based on the principles of welfare economics, see Brent, R.J. (2006), *Applied Cost-Benefit Analysis*, 2nd edition, Cheltenham UK and Northampton, MA, USA: Edward Elgar.

6. The full specification of the NHs on the GDS regression is equation (5) in Brent (2022), op. cit., and the results are in Table 3. The full specification of the NHs on the dementia symptoms regression is equation (7) and the results are in Table 4.

7. As we explained in the notes to the last chapter, including a set of constant terms for each visit number is a one-way, fixed effects strategy to establish causality. In our estimation we actually employed a two-way, fixed effects strategy by including a constant term for each individual, so "unobservables" that vary by individuals are controlled for, such as a person's personality type. In regression analysis, anything that is not included as an independent variable is an unobserved variable that could confound causality.

8. The parts of this chapter that cover the life expectancy losses from NHs is based on Brent, R.J. (2021a). "Life Expectancy in a Nursing Home", *Applied Economics*. doi: 10.1080/00036846.2021.1983138.

9. The particular survival estimation technique was the Weibull parametric model. This has the property that variables that change after the person goes into a NH model can also be included as part of the estimation of life expectancy. Equation (6) in Brent (2021a) gave the specification for the Weibull model. The controls in this equation were: age, gender, race, BMI, smoking years, currently taking any medications, Medicare eligibility, heart rate, and years of education.

10. Alzheimer's Association. "2018 Alzheimer's Disease Facts and Figures", *Alzheimer's Dementia*, 14, 367–429.

11. The VSLY in Chapter 5 was based on a VSL of $5.09 million related to Aldy and Viscusi's 2008 valuation. We used the updated value of $8.3 million to get $500,000 for a LY rather than $442,857 as in Chapter 5. This is because the base year for the VSL of NHs was 2016 and not 2008.

12. McCreedy, E.M., Weinstein, B.E., Chodosh, J., and Blustein, J. (2018), "Hearing Loss: Why Does It Matter for Nursing Homes?" *Journal of the American Medical Directors Association*, 19, 323–327.

13. Guoa, J., Konetzkab, T., and Manning, W.G. (2015), "The Causal Effects of Home Care Use on Institutional Long Term Care Utilization and Expenditures", *Health Economics*, 24(Suppl. 1), 4–17.

14. Hackmann, M.B. (2019), op. cit.

15. Aregay, A., O'Connor, M.O., Stow, J., Ayers, N., and Lee, S. (2020), "Strategies Used to Establish Palliative Care in Rural Low and Middle Income Countries: An Integrative Review", *Health Policy and Planning*, 35, 1110–1129.

16. World Health Organization (2017), "Towards Long Term Care Systems in Sub-Saharan African", *WHO Series on Long term Care*. License: CC BY-NC-SA 3.0 IGO.

17. Schell-Adlung, X. (2015), "Long Term Care Protection for Older Persons: A Review of Coverage Deficits in 46 countries", *International Labour*

Organization, ESS, Working Paper No. 50. The public long-term care percentages quoted in the text are listed in Figure 12.

18. Clausen, T., Wilson, A.O., Molebasti, R.M., and Holmboe-Ottesen, G. (2007), "Diminished Mental- and Physical Function and Lack of Social Support Are Associated with Shorter Survival in Community Dwelling Older Persons of Botswana", *Bio Med Central*, 7, 144 (8 pages).

19. World Health Organization (2017), op. cit., section 2.3.4.

PART III

Public policy implications of dementia interventions

8. Elder abuse

We have just seen that older adults in NHs have not been given better care than they would have received if they had not entered NHs. Residents enter NHs with the expectation that they would obtain better care, not worse care. There is usually an element of trust involved by residents in their caregivers. When caregivers for the elderly violate that trust, then elder abuse can be said to have taken place. This is a generally valid principle for the elderly, both within and outside NHs, that trust has to be involved and violated for elder abuse to be said to exist.[1] By definition, people with dementia have difficulties with activities of daily living and so they rely on others for assistance. This fact, and their vulnerability, make persons with dementia more likely to experience elder abuse than other older adults. Because of this, an intervention for reducing dementia can also be thought of as an intervention for reducing elder abuse. As we shall see, there are large monetary benefits from reducing elder abuse. This means that all five of the dementia interventions that have been evaluated, by subsequently reducing the possibility of elder abuse, will have even more benefits than have been attributed to them so far.

CHAPTER OUTLINE

There are four main types of elder abuse: physical, psychological, financial, and neglect. Sexual elder abuse can be a fifth type, but it is often subsumed under the physical abuse category. We are going to value all four types of elder abuse in this chapter. We will apply a different method for estimating the benefits of preventing elder abuse neglect from the other three types. This is because the existence of neglect is often harder to prove. So, we will present a new, three-part test to establish the presence of elder abuse neglect. We will also refer to a different data set for the estimation of the benefits of the three non-neglect elder abuse types, since the NACC data set does not explicitly deal with elder abuse. However, we can still use the NACC data set to help value neglect, as it provides evidence of the extent of any neglect that is uncovered (part three of the elder abuse neglect test).

We start with an introduction to elder abuse by presenting the main characteristics of the four types and give some estimates of the prevalence for each type in the general population, and especially for those with dementia. The extent of underreporting of elder abuse is emphasized. We then turn to the issue of how to quantify the degrees of severity posed by the various kinds of elder abuse, in order that a meaningful unit can be defined for making benefit valuations. Two specifications are presented. The first is used to value physical, psychological, and financial elder abuse in which the criminal justice system is involved. The second specification is used to value elder abuse neglect. Since neglect is the most underreported type of elder abuse, a three-part test procedure for detecting elder abuse is outlined. This test procedure is then applied to the non-provision of HAs in nursing homes, so that this example of elder abuse neglect can be valued per person and for the entire US population.

In the next section, when interventions for elder abuse are being discussed, the focus will be exclusively on multidimensional interventions, as these are the main ones that have been found to be effective. Since there are no CBAs of an elder abuse intervention in the literature, a CBA will be created for an important multidimensional intervention called the Elder Abuse Forensic Center (EAFC) model. This evaluation will use the benefit estimates derived in the context of the criminal justice system and compare them with the costs of the EAFC that have been recently estimated in the literature. After the section examining the relevance of elder abuse interventions for LMICs, we close with the summary and conclusions.

CHARACTERISTICS OF ELDER ABUSE

Table 8.1 lists the main types of elder abuse, explaining the symptoms, and showing how the outcomes of elder abuse can be quantified.[2]

Much of this chapter will be devoted to providing a deeper understanding and valuation of the content in Table 8.1. In particular, "harassment" will be the benchmark for estimating the benefits of preventing physical and sexual, psychological, and financial abuse; and the "absence of aids" (specifically, hearing aids) will be the benchmark for estimating the benefits of elder abuse neglect. Note also that for neglect, the table specifies the failure to provide appropriate "activities of daily living" and the inability to carry out ADLs was our definition of dementia. So dementia is inextricably linked to elder abuse neglect.

Table 8.1   *Elder abuse typologies, possible manifestations and potential indicators*

Type of Abuse	Possible Manifestations	Potential Indicators
Physical	Hitting, slapping, pushing, kicking, medication misuse, force feeding, inappropriate sanctions, restraint.	Bruising, cuts, scratches, hair loss, lacerations, missing teeth, fractures, kick marks, eye injuries, burns.
Sexual	Rape, sexual assaults or acts the older person has not consented to, or has not the ability to consent to.	Trauma around the genitals, breasts, rectum or mouth.
Psychological	Humiliation, intimidation, threats of abandonment, ridicule, causing fear/ anxiety, verbal abuse, harassment, withholding social contact, denial of basic rights.	Demoralization, depression, withdrawal, apathy, feeling hopeless, insomnia, appetite change, paranoia, agitation, tearfulness, excessive fears, confusion.
Financial	Sudden reduction in financial funds, removal of material property, coerced signing over of property/funds/ material goods, or changes of will.	Disappearance of property, absence of required aids or medication, refusal to spend money, disparity of assets and living conditions, dramatic financial decisions.
Neglect	Ignoring physical/medical needs, failure to provide appropriate services of life and/or activities of daily living (such as medication, heating).	Dehydration, malnutrition, inappropriate clothing, poor hygiene, over-/ undermedicated, exposure to risk/ danger, absence of aids (Zimmer frame, reading glasses), pressure sores.

Source: Based on Table 1.1 in Phelan (2013), op. cit.

PREVALENCE OF ELDER ABUSE

In a review of national surveys of the one-year prevalence of all forms of elder abuse, three summary estimates were highlighted. The rates were 7.6 percent, 9 percent, and 10 percent, On the basis of these three epidemiological studies of community dwelling older adults, the conclusion was that an overall prevalence estimate of 10 percent for elder abuse would be reasonable.[3]

These estimates mostly relied on officially documented cases that were referred to social service, law enforcement, or legal authorities who are responsible for assisting older adult victims. However, based on self-reported data, a New York State study found that the incidence rate (new cases) of financial abuse was 42.1 per 1,000 adults over the age of 60; the rate was 22.4 for physical and sexual abuse; it was 18.3

for neglect, and 16.4 for psychological abuse. What was striking about these self-reported incidence rates of elder abuse was that they were on average nearly 24 times greater than the official rates. The self-reported rate for neglect was 57.2 times greater and was the most underreported type of elder abuse. This gross, official underreporting means that much of the elder abuse that exists remains hidden and can be called "under the radar."[4]

PREVALENCE OF ELDER ABUSE WITH PERSONS OF DEMENTIA[5]

If 10 percent is the typical elder abuse prevalence rate for all older adults, then the prevalence rate for those with dementia is much higher. The prevalence rates for those with dementia range from 27.9 percent to 62.3 percent.[6] Psychological abuse was consistently the most prevalent form of elder abuse of people with dementia.

The higher prevalence rates for those with dementia are understandable (though not justified) given that older persons with dementia are more vulnerable to elder abuse than are older adults without dementia. This mainly arises out of the fact that persons with dementia are more dependent on others for their care. We have seen that difficulties with decision-making, in terms of judgment and problem solving, was a key component of the CDR instrument that we have been using to quantify the extent of dementia symptoms in this book. So passing financial decision-making responsibilities on to others, by allowing others to manage one's financial affairs, is bound to leave a person with dementia especially vulnerable to financial elder abuse. Since the person with dementia is likely to be unaware of the financial abuse, it is not surprising that financial elder abuse is both widespread and underreported for those with dementia.

The higher prevalence rate of elder abuse among those with dementia occurs both in and outside NHs. Inside NHs, nurses are not always aware of the special needs of those with dementia. Nurses are also often unaware that their actions constitute elder abuse and they need to be educated about this. Outside NHs, where care is undertaken by the family, elder abuse would be expected to be higher because caring for someone with dementia creates more stress on the caregiver, especially if the person with dementia's behavior is aggressive.

QUANTIFYING ELDER ABUSE

From the point of view of valuing the benefits of preventing elder abuse, there is an immediate problem involved with the quantification of the extent of elder abuse using data coming from the literature. To estimate the benefits of an intervention, one needs a meaningful unit of outcome on which to place a valuation. The literature simply adds cases without reference to the severity of the cases. In terms of Table 8.1, the literature is effectively simply adding up, in any particular setting, the number of cases of slapping, the number of rapes, and the number of pressure sores that took place to produce the total number of elder abuse cases that were perpetrated. Clearly, these offenses are not of equal importance. Slapping is not acceptable; but is not of the same order of magnitude as rape, from which some women never fully recover, and pressure sores that, as we saw in the last chapter, could be fatal.

There are two possible solutions to this aggregation problem as to how to count cases when the severity of offenses are unequal. One is to apply a measure of severity to each offense, so that when adjusted by severity, the cases are made comparable for valuation purposes. The other solution is to select one particular offense, whose severity can be somewhat readily understood and valued, and then see how prevalent that one case of elder abuse is in the population. In this solution, no attempt is made to compare offenses of different severity. In our estimation of the benefits of preventing elder abuse in this chapter we will adopt both solutions; the first solution for physical, psychological, and financial abuse, and the second solution for elder abuse neglect.

VALUING PHYSICAL, PSYCHOLOGICAL, AND FINANCIAL ABUSE[7]

In economics, the standard way for valuing severity, that is, expressing the strength of preferences for any good or service, is to find out what a person is willing to pay for it. In neither the economics literature nor the health literature generally is there a study that tries to estimate the willingness to pay for the prevention of a case of any type of elder abuse by the victim. But there does exist a study, based on a book from the elder abuse literature in the context of the criminal justice system, which does come up with a meaningful measure of the severity of the main types of elder abuse.[8] The data source for this study was not from the NACC as it was collected separately.[9]

When elder abuse has taken place and brought to the attention of the police, a standardized procedure was adopted. After the police arrive at the location of the elder abuse, they try to establish the specifics of the offense, in terms of who was the perpetrator (age, gender, race), who was the victim (age, gender, race), and the details of the offense, which they then classified (such as petty larceny, harassment, and assault). They also try to record a monetary amount for the offense, especially if financial abuse was involved. The police report culminated in an outcome expressed in terms of whether the victim was willing to prosecute the perpetrator. Now it must be understood that the perpetrator was in all instances a family member of an older adult and thus in a position of trust. Therefore, by definition, elder abuse was the offense in all cases. The data details were as follows.

There were 257 police reports, based on 17 categories of offense; 72 percent of the victims were willing to prosecute the perpetrator; the victim's age on average was 69 years and the perpetrator's age was 34 years; 71 percent of the victims were women and 78 percent of the perpetrators were men. Slightly above half of the victims and perpetrators were black. In 58 percent of the cases, the victim and perpetrator lived together.

Whether to prosecute the perpetrator posed an enormous dilemma for the victim. The family member may also be a caregiver and a loved one, so sending the perpetrator to prison is not something to be taken lightly. On the other hand, if the elder abuse by the family member was judged to be so very serious by the victim that it had to stop, such as a case of rape, then prosecuting the perpetrator would at least prevent the elder abuse from continuing. Some restitution may also take place if financial abuse was the offense. Overall, then, the decision whether to prosecute the perpetrator revealed the seriousness of the offense in the eyes of the person most affected by the elder abuse, that is, the victim.

The first task was therefore to take the prosecution percentages for each of the 17 offenses used to classify a case by the police and then rank them in order to identify the seriousness of the offenses from the point of view of the victim. The highest prosecution percentage was 100 for menacing and the lowest percentage was 27 for family disputes. In between the upper and lower bounds was harassment at 65 percent, which was close to the average of 72 percent for all prosecutions. From this ranking of the seriousness of offenses, two classes were constructed: "serious offenses" were those offenses that had prosecution percentages above

80; and "non-serious offenses" were those offenses that had prosecution percentages below 80. This meant that there was now a unit of account (serious/non-serious) that could be used to value the elder abuse cases. In effect, a charge of harassment can be thought of as the benchmark for a classification of a non-serious offense.

The serious offenses were then broken down into two categories, financial and non-financial. This was because financial elder abuse was the foundation stone for the valuation of all offenses. Cases that involve financial abuse as an offense have automatically built into them both a monetary measurement and a degree of seriousness, that is, the amount of money that is taken from the complainant. So $1,000 extorted is clearly going to be more serious than financial abuse that expropriates $100, and this in turn is going to be more serious than an offense involving the theft of $10. Once serious financial offenses were valued, the values for the non-financial serious offenses could be set by comparing them by their relative importance to the financial serious offenses in the victim's decision whether to prosecute or not. This explains the logic of the method. We now give the estimation results.

The complete analysis can be condensed into two regression equations. In the first, the dependent variable was a dummy variable that took the value of 1 if the victim judged that the offense was to be classed as a serious case of financial elder abuse (that is, in the top 80 percent of offenses that victims were willing to prosecute) and zero otherwise. The main independent variable was the amount of the financial abuse in the charge statement. The controls were how the complaint was initiated (called in, or by attending the police station) and whether the precinct contacted had the most offenses.[10] Thus, this regression tells us how much must be at stake financially for the charge to be classed as a serious case of elder abuse. The result was that it took around $40,000 for the financial offense to change the dependent variable from 0 to 1 and become a serious financial offense.

In the second regression, the dependent variable was the willingness to prosecute, again a dummy variable that took the value of 1 if the victim was willing to prosecute and zero otherwise. The two main independent variables (together with the controls involving race and whether the victim and perpetrator lived together) were whether the case was a serious financial offense or a serious non-financial offense.[11] The ratio of the coefficients of the two types of offense in this regression indicates how much the impact of one category of offense was judged important, relative to the other category of offense in the decision whether to prosecute or not. It turned out that the ratio was around 1.26.[12] This meant that a serious non-financial offense was valued 1.26 times greater than a serious financial offense, which from the first regression was valued at $40,000. The result was that a serious non-financial offense was valued at around $50,000.

VALUING ELDER ABUSE NEGLECT[13]

Valuing elder abuse neglect is more difficult than valuing the other types of elder abuse because it is harder to establish that a case of neglect has taken place. The other types of elder abuse, physical, psychological, and financial, are also underreported, but at least there can be visible signs of their abuse. A bruise and a fracture can be diagnosed, and an empty bank account can be detected. But, how does one observe something that did not take place that should have taken place, which neglect involves? So elder abuse neglect is inherently more difficult to quantify than the other types of abuse. This is an important reason why neglect is so much more underreported. Because of this fact, a different, layered strategy for detecting elder abuse neglect has to be adopted. Only when a case has been reliably detected can it then be valued.

The strategy that we will be using to detect elder abuse neglect is based on a test that has three parts. First, it must be demonstrated that what the caregiver is not providing is a need for the older adult. Second, what is needed should be something that is socially worthwhile. Third, what is needed and socially worthwhile has to be shown to be something that has been deprived from the older adult.

We will apply the test to hearing aids in nursing homes, as we have covered both HAs and NHs as dementia interventions in previous chapters. So the dementia connection has already been established. What we are now going to analyse is the extent to which NHs, in addition to increasing dementia symptoms, are also detrimental by contributing to elder abuse neglect. We will run each of the three steps for the detection test in turn based on the NACC data set.

- Checking whether HAs are needed: The most obvious reason why an HA would pass a test of being needed is that on the basis of a hearing exam, the verdict was that the person has HL that an HA would remedy.[14] In the part of the NACC data set we will be using to detect elder abuse, everyone has had a hearing exam and found to have HL. So everyone was in need of an HA.

- Checking whether HAs are worthwhile: In Chapter 5 we covered in great detail the evaluation of HAs, which showed that the total benefits were nearly 30 times greater than the costs. Even when just dealing with the indirect benefits involved with the impact of HAs in reducing dementia symptoms, the benefits were 1.2 times greater than the costs. There can therefore be no doubt that an HA is very socially worthwhile when it can be used by a NH resident.
- Checking whether residents are being deprived of HAs: In the NACC data set, 60 percent of older adults with HL used HAs. This was because only 1 percent of older adults lived in NHs. Wearing an HA outside a NH was their choice. When living in NHs, residents' usage of HAs was reduced by one-sixth. This estimate was obtained by regressing living in a NH (and the usual controls) against HA usage (usually wearing an HA or not) and the coefficient was –0.167.[15] NHs were significantly denying HA use.

Using our one-sixth estimate of neglect and the net-benefits value for HAs, we can provide an approximate national assessment of the scope and value lost by elder abuse neglect. In the USA, there are around 1,108,610 long-stay NH residents, 32 percent of which had some HL.[16] This means that there were around 354,755 persons at risk of neglect. Taking one-sixth of this number to be actually validated cases of negligent abuse, this means that the number subject to elder abuse neglect from the non-provision of HAs at NHs was 59,244.

To put a monetary value on the number of negligent cases in NHs, we need to adjust the net-benefit estimate of HAs of $239,927 in Chapter 5 to allow for the fact that residents in NHs have a shorter life expectancy and they are more likely to have dementia. With these adjustments, the net-benefits estimate became $74,708 per person.[17] Multiplying this sum by the 59,244 persons estimated to have been affected by neglect results in a $4.4 billion projected loss of benefits from HA neglect in NHs in the USA.

Now that the loss of benefits from all the main types of elder abuse have been estimated, we can now turn our attention to what can be done about reducing these losses.

INTERVENTIONS FOR REDUCING ELDER ABUSE

In a 2009 survey of elder abuse interventions, the conclusion was that: "there is currently insufficient evidence to support any particular intervention related to elder abuse targeting clients, perpetrators, or health care professionals."[18]

However, more recently there seems to be a consensus in the elder abuse literature that any effective intervention for elder abuse must take a comprehensive multidisciplinary approach.[19] This makes sense, as elder abuse itself is a complex, multidimensional phenomenon. As an illustration of what such an approach entails, we can refer to the Israeli multisystem model for the treatment and prevention of elder abuse in the community.[20]

The Israeli model originated in three municipalities between the years 2005 and 2007. It started with setting up a Specialized Unit for the Prevention and Treatment of Elder Abuse (SUPTEA). This had a social worker as a coordinator, and had a paraprofessional assistant and a multi-disciplinary advisory team. The paraprofessional made home visits and follow-up visits, and accompanied older people for medical check-ups. The advisory team shared information and expertise, discussed complex cases, and developed an intervention plan. The two main activities were casework (including individual counseling, mediation, and referrals for appropriate services, and legal actions such as the appointment of legal guardianship) and community work (raising community awareness and including educational workshops in day-care centers, seniors' clubs, and conferences for professionals).

The multidimensional interventions were shown to be effective for all the main types of elder abuse, as assessed by social workers based on client reports, in terms of the extent to which there had been a change in the abusive situation in the last six months. In two-thirds of the cases, the situation had improved (by 63 percent for psychological abuse, by 61 percent for physical abuse, by 66 percent for financial abuse, and 72 percent for neglect).

A CBA OF A MULTIDIMENSIONAL ELDER ABUSE INTERVENTION

We have just seen that the elder abuse literature does contain examples of effective interventions. What is missing from this literature is an evaluation of any existing effective intervention to ascertain whether it was socially worthwhile. To help remedy this deficiency, we will construct the beginnings of a CBA of an existing elder abuse intervention. Our illustrative CBA combines the benefit estimates presented earlier in this chapter with the cost estimates for an effective intervention in the literature.[21] The intervention is called the Elder Abuse Forensic Center (EAFC) model that was implemented in Los Angeles. It was set up to deal with the most serious cases of elder abuse.

The EAFC model brings together diverse professionals from a variety of fields within the justice system, health care, protective services, and mental health. What is distinctive about the EAFC from other multidisciplinary teams is that it has a greater array of disciplines involved. For instance, the EAFC contains: a Geriatrician, Adult Protective Services (APS), an Ombudsman, a Public Guardian, a Real Estate District Attorney, and Free Legal Aid for Seniors. What is also distinctive is that the EAFC is more action focused and is task orientated. The teams meet every week, devise a plan of action, and team members assist in carrying out the recommendations.[22]

The outcome of the EAFC intervention that we will be focusing on for the evaluation is an additional serious case of elder abuse that is prosecuted by the District Attorney's Office (DAO). The majority of cases that are prosecuted by the DAO attain a plea or conviction. We previously learned of the estimated value to a victim for prosecuting each of the two main categories of serious elder abuse. Therefore, what is needed now, for the CBA to be carried out, is for the cost of getting a case prosecuted to be determined, and a comparison intervention to be specified in order to see if the EAFC is more worthwhile than an alternative intervention. The main costing method was to take the number of hours spent on a case prepared for prosecution and multiply this by the salaries of the persons dealing with the case. The comparison group was a case that was sent to the DAO by APS.

The causality strategy that was adopted for estimating the costs per case prosecuted is the standard one used by medical researchers in the form of a randomized clinical trial. There is a treatment group (the EAFC), where cases are randomly assigned, and a comparison control group (the APS), where cases are also randomly assigned. If the two sets of cases have been truly randomized, there should be no difference in the cost per prosecution in terms of age, race, gender, and so on. Any difference in costs per case prosecuted between the two groups should then only be because one came from the EAFC group and the other came from the APS group.[23]

The main cost finding was that it took more time to process a case with the EAFC group (10.36 hours versus 3.72 hours) and so it cost more overall per prosecution than for the APS group ($1,108.80 versus $153.30). For this additional cost investment, the prosecution rate outcome was 17 percent higher with the EAFC group. This translated into an additional cost of $7,414.52 per serious case of elder abuse prosecuted by the DAO (and an additional cost of $8,731.40 per successful prosecution).

The resulting CBA would proceed as follows. The benefits from prosecuting a serious case of non-financial elder abuse were around $50,000. At a cost of around $7,500, this produces positive net-benefits of $42,500 and a benefit-cost ratio of 6.67. For a serious case of financial abuse, the benefit was around $40,000. Subtracting the same $7,500 cost figure makes the net-benefits positive at $32,500 with a benefit-cost ratio of 5.33. Interventions for elder abuse via the criminal justice system therefore appear to be very socially worthwhile.

ELDER ABUSE AND LMICS

It would be an accurate statement to say that the prevalence of elder abuse in LMICs is unknown. It is not simply the case that the numbers are underreported, which is true of the USA; it is the fact that they are not reported at all. The failure to report data on financial elder abuse in LMICs can itself be interpreted to be evidence of elder abuse, as this quote from a recent study on financial abuse in LMICs confirms, "The absence of data on the prevalence and severity of financial abuse does not indicate that the problem is negligible; only that it is being neglected."[24]

Nonetheless, there does exist in the elder abuse literature some corroborative evidence related to LMICs that older adults feel vulnerable to crime generally, and not just the crime of elder abuse related to people that are trusted like family members. Numerous studies show that the fear of crime can affect the behavior of older adults in terms of limiting mobility and social participation, which we have seen are symptoms of dementia. A recent study of adults aged 50 and older in six LMICs (India, China, Ghana, Mexico, Russia, and Mexico) found that when asked about feelings of safety alone at home, the average home fear was 13.4 percent; and when asked about feelings of safety on streets alone after dark, the average street fear was 25.7 percent.[25] Fear of crime was high overall and had two main characteristics:

- Women's home and street fear was higher than that for males (14.6 percent relative to percent for home fear, and 29.8 percent relative to 19.4 percent for street fear); and

- Country variation was even larger (South Africa had 46.9 percent for home fear and 64.6 percent for street fear, while Ghana had 4.9 percent for home fear and 8.6 percent for street fear).

In the absence of large-scale, national studies of financial elder abuse in LMICs, a South African case study related to one particular, generally relevant, LMIC type of financial abuse could be informative.[26] The elder abuse in question occurs whenever a person is being coerced to share old age pensions with the rest of the family. Old age pensions were selected for analysis as they are a major source of security for older adults in many LMICs, and are widely advocated as a way of increasing QoL in later life. Pooling of pensions is widespread in LDCs. Some of the sharing is mutually beneficial. Nevertheless, many times the older adult is forced to share without their consent. One study in the Eastern Cape of South Africa found that over 40 percent of respondents reported that none of their pension income was reserved for their own personal use. The policy concern raised by the case study is that, when in the future data is collected, one needs to be able to distinguish pension pooling that is consensual from that which is not. This is likely to be a challenging exercise, especially if the dependent elder is cognitively impaired.

At this time, one would have to conclude that it is premature to advocate multidisciplinary elder abuse interventions for LMICs, like the EAFC model that was found worthwhile in the USA. This is simply because elder abuse agencies in LMICs have to first exist for them subsequently to be coordinated.[27]

SUMMARY AND CONCLUSIONS

There are four main types of elder abuse; physical, psychological, financial, and neglect. The presence of elder abuse is believed to be high, especially as there is widespread evidence of an underreporting of cases. The data reveal that the prevalence of elder abuse is even higher in older adults with dementia.

Because there is large underreporting of elder abuse, especially for neglect, a three-part test for detecting neglect was devised. An ADL must be needed, worthwhile, and deprived from an older adult. All three tests were passed to confirm that there has been significant HAs neglect in NHs in the USA. Older adults living outside NHs were able to choose to use HAs one-sixth times greater than when living in NHs.

The monetary benefits of preventing elder abuse are substantial. Combining physical and psychological elder abuse, the estimate was around $50,000, and for financial elder abuse, it was around $40,000 per episode. Preventing elder abuse neglect by not providing HAs in NHs was estimated to be $74,708 per person, which amounted to $4.4 billion when aggregated across all older persons living in NHs in the USA.

All our estimates incorporated the consumer sovereignty value judgment (the individual is the best judge of their own welfare) that is used as the welfare economic base behind measuring benefits in CBA. For physical, psychological, and financial abuse, it was a victim's intensity of preferences in terms of their willingness to prosecute the perpetrator that was used to estimate benefits. For elder abuse neglect, it was the victim's preferences for using HAs which was used to estimate benefits. Using HAs was their own choice when living outside a NH, but using HAs was mainly the caregiver's choice in NHs.

The importance of respecting an older person's preferences when evaluating interventions was dramatically illustrated in the case of financial abuse. Financial elder abuse has a built-in monetary valuation, being the amount of money involved with the offense. Although the average size of a financial offense was only around $2,547 in the sample, it took around $40,000 in order for it to be classed as a serious financial offense. To an outsider, it would be reported that on average $2,547 was stolen from an older adult victim in the sample.

However, to an insider, the victim themself, the pain, suffering, and humiliation from knowing that it was a family member that stole that $2,547 was valued at around $40,000.

Very few studies in the elder abuse literature identified effective interventions. When they were identified, and multidimensional interventions were the main type of elder abuse intervention that were found to be effective, only recently have costs been estimated as part of the evaluation. Thus, it should not be surprising that no CBA of an elder abuse intervention existed in the literature for us to present and analyse.[28]

To remedy this omission, we created the beginnings of a CBA by combining our estimates of the benefits of prosecuting perpetrators with the costs of prosecuting perpetrators in the literature. The intervention that was costed was a multiservice intervention called the EAFC model. What makes an elder abuse intervention multidimensional is that it integrates three main sets of workers, that is, medical (including mental health), social workers, and members of the criminal justice system. What makes the EAFC model so distinctive is the comprehensiveness to which it integrates the three sets of workers. The purported CBA of the EAFC model found that it was highly worthwhile, with net-benefits of \$32,500 per case prosecuted and a benefit-cost ratio of 5.33. With this beginning of a CBA, with the benefits of persons from New York and the costs from persons in Los Angeles, the literature has something to build on and develop.

Given that:

- In this chapter it has been found that having dementia makes one vulnerable for elder abuse, and reducing elder abuse has monetary rewards; and
- In previous chapters, it has been found that reducing dementia also has monetary rewards, it follows that:
- If one implements interventions that reduce dementia symptoms, one must add the two sets or rewards to obtain the total benefits of the dementia interventions.

This makes the value of the dementia interventions evaluated in this book become even more valuable than we have assigned them earlier. In economics, when the effect of one intervention affects the effect of another intervention indirectly, the interaction is called an externality. One can therefore say that a dementia intervention has an external benefit for evaluating an elder abuse intervention, in that if one can prevent dementia symptoms one will also be reducing the opportunity for elder abuse.

Almost all the literature on elder abuse emphasizes the fact that these abuses are illegal. This opens up the whole issue of the importance of instituting laws and conventions to protect the human rights of older adults. Examining the value of protecting the human rights of older adults is the subject matter of the next and final chapter of the book.

NOTES

1. Bonnie, R.J. and Wallace, R.B. (2002), *Elder Mistreatment: Abuse, Neglect and Exploitation in an Aging America*, 39–41, Washington, DC: National Academies Press.
2. Phelan, A., ed. (2013), "International Perspectives on Elder Abuse", in *Elder Abuse – an Introduction*, London and New York: Routledge, pp. 1–31.
3. Lachs, M. and Pillemer, K.A. (2015), "Elder Abuse", *The New England Journal of Medicine*, 373, 1947–1956.
4. Lachs, M. and Berman, J. (2011), *Under the Radar: New York State Elder Abuse Prevalence Study.* Final Report. Prepared by: Lifespan of Greater

Rochester, Inc., Weill Cornell Medical Center of Cornell University and New York City Department for the Aging.

5. This section is based on Downes, C., Fealy, G., Phelan, A., Donnelly, N., and Lafferty, A. (2013), *Abuse of Older People with Dementia: A Review*, National Centre for Older Persons (NCPOP), University College Dublin.

6. Phelan. A. (2015), "Protecting Care Home Residents from Mistreatment and Abuse: On the Need for Policy", *Risk Management and Healthcare Policy*, 8, 215–223.

7. The parts of this chapter valuing elder abuse related to the criminal justice system are based on Brent, R.J. (2015), "Valuing the Prevention of Elder Abuse", *Applied Economics*, 47, 6362–6373.

8. The book on which Brent (2015), ibid., was based was Brownell, P. (1998), *Family Crimes Against the Elderly: Elder Abuse and the Criminal Justice System*, New York: Garland Publishing.

9. Many thanks to Professor Pat Brownell for sharing her data with me so that I could undertake my study.

10. The first regression is equation (11) in Brent (2015), op. cit., and the results are in Table 6 estimated by Ordinary Least Squares.

11. The second regression is equation (2) in Brent (2015), op. cit., and the results are in Table 5. As was pointed out in note 10 in chapter 6, when the dependent variable in a regression equation is a dummy variable, then dichotomous regression estimation techniques must be employed. In this case, Probit was the estimation technique used.

12. Finding a ratio >1 in the regression, that a non-financial serious offense was valued more highly than a financial serious offense, makes sense as the willingness to prosecute percentage was higher for the non-financial serious offenses (89 percent or 90 percent as opposed to 83 percent for financial offenses).

13. The parts of this chapter valuing elder abuse neglect related to HAs in NHs are based on Brent, R.J. (2021b), "Detecting the Incidence and Benefits Foregone of Elder Abuse Neglect: The Case of Hearing Aids in Nursing Homes", *Review of Economics and Finance*, 19, 1–8.

14. There is a much more general criterion for judging any kind of need for an older adult in the context of neglect, and that is whether the caregiver provides the necessary activities of daily living (ADL), see Brent (2021b), op. cit. The ADL that is relevant for HAs is the need to communicate, and HL has been shown to disrupt communication.

15. With the dependent variable also being a dummy variable, Probit was again the regression estimation technique used. The full specification of the HA use regression is equation (1) of Brent (2021b), op. cit., and the results are in Table 4.

16. McCreedy, E.M., Weinstein, B.E., Chodosh, J., and Blustein, J. (2018), "Hearing Loss: Why Does It Matter for Nursing Homes?" *Journal of the American Medical Directors Association*, 19, 323–327.

17. The adjustment was made as follows. The net-benefits for those without dementia were shown in Chapter 5 to be $239,927. The life years used in the CBA was 23 for this group. The LY were 17.9 years in US NHs.

Scaling back the net-benefits for the 78 percent duration in NHs produces a $186,726 figure for this group. For those with dementia, the scaling back has to be much larger. They survived only 1.33 years. With a 94 percent shorter duration, the net-benefits for the dementia group would have been $14,396. Since 65 percent of the residents in NHs have dementia, a weighted average of the two groups benefits amounts to $74,708 per person.

18. Ploeg, J., Fear, J., Hutchison, B., MacMillan, and Bolan, G. (2009), "A Systematic Review of Interventions for Elder Abuse", *Journal of Elder Abuse and Neglect*, 21, 1–34.

19. See, for example, Phelan, A. (2015), op. cit., and Pillemer, K., Burnes, D., Riffin, C., and Lachs, M.S. (2016), "Elder Abuse: Global Situation, Risk Factors, and Prevention Strategies", *The Gerontologist*, 56, S194–S205.

20. Alon, S. and Berg-Warman, A. (2014), "Treatment and Prevention of Elder Abuse and Neglect: Where Knowledge and Practice Meet – a Model for Intervention to Prevent Elder Treatment in Israel", *Journal of Elder Abuse and Neglect*, 26, 150–171.

21. Nichol, M.B., Wilber, K.H., Wu, J., and Gassoumis, Z.D. (2015), "Evaluating the Cost Effectiveness of the Elder Abuse Forensic Center Model", *Report Submitted to the US Department of Justice*.

22. Schneider, D.C., Mosqueta, L., Falk, E., and Huba, G.J. (2010), "Elder Abuse Forensic Centers", *Journal of Elder Abuse and Neglect*, 22, 255–274.

23. In the case of the Nichol et al. (2015) study, op. cit., they did not rely purely on random assignment to ensure that the treatment and controls were comparable preintervention, as they used propensity score matching to achieve comparability.

24. Lloyd-Sherlock, P., Penhale, B., and Ayiga, N. (2018), "Financial Abuse of Older People in Low and Middle-Income Countries: The Case of South Africa", *Journal of Elder Abuse and Neglect*, 30, 236–246.

25. Lloyd-Sherlock, P., Agrawal, S., and Minicuci, N. (2016), "Fear of Crime and Older People in Low- and Middle-Income Countries", *Ageing and Society*, 36, 1083–1108.

26. Lloyd-Sherlock et al. (2018), op. cit.

27. Pillemer, K., Bumes, D., Riffin, C., and Lachs, M.S. (2016), "Elder Abuse: Global Situation, Risk Factors, and Prevention Strategies", *The Gerontologist*, 56, S194–S204.

28. Since no CBAs of elder abuse interventions exist for any older persons, it follows that no elder abuse interventions exist for older persons with dementia. However, an effectiveness study for an elder abuse intervention for persons with dementia does exist and, not surprisingly, it is a multiservice intervention, which features a handbook for caregivers. See Anetzberger, G.J., Palmisano, B.R., Sanders, M., Bass, D., Dayton, C., Eckert, S., and Schimer, M.R. (2000), "A Model Intervention for Elder Abuse and Dementia", *The Gerontologist*, 40, 492–497. This study also confirms the high prevalence rates for elder abuse for those with dementia.

9.   Human rights

We have just seen that older persons with dementia are subject to elder abuse, which is illegal. The intervention we evaluated was ensuring that persons would be prosecuted under the law. In this chapter, we analyse the laws themselves as interventions. In particular, we focus on laws that need to apply to all older adults with dementia irrespective of which country they live in.

What is relevant in this context is the existence and implementation of United Nations (UN) conventions/treaties that address the human rights of all older persons with dementia.

The starting point for recent human rights statements is the Universal Declaration of Human Rights (1948). Everyone is supposed to receive equal human rights under the law no matter a person's age or health state. It turns out that those with disabilities felt that they had been excluded from the implementation of these universal human rights. So a separate treaty was initiated called the UN Convention on the Rights of Persons with Disabilities (2006). Since dementia is a special kind of disability, it was hoped that older persons with dementia would now have their rights protected. However, as we saw in the last chapter, older persons are subject to widespread elder abuse, and older adults with dementia are especially victimized. In this chapter, we provide additional evidence of financial abuse in the form of inadequate social protection. If older adults as a group are not being protected, then older adults with dementia, who are a sub-group, are not being protected. It is therefore time for a new convention to be confirmed, one that explicitly refers to older adults and includes special provisions for older adults with dementia. With a new convention for older adults, the financing of all the socially worthwhile interventions evaluated in this book would become a public policy priority.

CHAPTER OUTLINE

We begin our analysis of human rights conventions in their role of promoting the provision of social protection for older persons by summarizing the two main conventions in this regard, with special emphasis on people with dementia. We then look at some empirical evidence as to whether existing social protection programs in the form of pensions have been successfully implemented. We find existing social protection lacking. The need for a new convention for the rights of older persons is promoted and what such a new convention possibly should contain is indicated.

An intervention for persons with dementia that is explicitly specified as a human right involves cognitive rehabilitation (CR). A section is therefore devoted to explaining the essentials of this intervention. As the main version of CR is called the Tailored Activity Program (TAP), we carry out an economic evaluation of this intervention. The standard three-step method for estimating the benefits of any intervention is applied to TAP. Once the costs of TAP are identified, the CBA can take place. TAP will also be the focus of the section dealing with the relevance of CR evaluations for LMICs.

As this is the final chapter of the book, we close with two summary and conclusions sections, one for this chapter on human rights, and one for the book as a whole.

INTERNATIONAL TREATIES FOR HUMAN RIGHTS FOR THOSE WITH DEMENTIA

International treaties/conventions lay out the agenda for universal rights and consequential policies for older persons with dementia. The starting point is the Universal Declaration of Human Rights (1948). The key provision is Article 25(1) that states:[1]

> Everyone has the right to a standard of living adequate for the health and well-being of himself and of his family, including food, clothing, housing and medical care and necessary social services, and the right to security in the event of unemployment, sickness, disability, widowhood, old age or other lack of livelihood in circumstances beyond his control.

This provision was specified to be universal. It should therefore include older adults with dementia, especially as it explicitly states that health and well-being must relate to "old age." In addition, the provision is comprehensive covering "housing and medical care and necessary social services" that dementia patients require, and including a person's "family," which could be the person's caregiver.

It is important to recognize that this 1948 convention article also explicitly refers to persons with "disability." The human rights of persons with disability are to be protected under the convention. Therefore, the fact that the UN itself subsequently considered it necessary to introduce an additional convention for those with disabilities is conclusive proof that the 1948 convention did not, in practice, protect the rights for all persons. The UN did not think that simply stating that "everyone" has rights meant that persons with disabilities had their rights protected. So a second convention was adopted just for those with disability called the UN Convention on the Rights of Persons with Disabilities (2006). The opening article states:[2]

> The purpose of the present Convention is to promote, protect and ensure the full and equal enjoyment of all human rights and fundamental freedoms by all persons with disabilities, and to promote respect for their inherent dignity. Persons with disabilities include those who have long term physical, mental, intellectual or sensory impairments which in interaction with various barriers may hinder their full and effective participation in society on an equal basis with others.

Since, under the second convention, long-term "mental" health is specified as a disability, one could be lulled into thinking that the human rights of older adults with dementia are now fully protected with these two conventions in place. Let us see what the data reveal on this issue.

THE NEED FOR A NEW, SEPARATE HUMAN RIGHTS CONVENTION FOR OLDER ADULTS

Although we have just seen that two UN Human Rights conventions do exist for older adults and those with dementia, they are insufficient to provide social protection in practice for these groups. In all countries, most older adults do not work, and most persons with dementia rely on caregivers. Although older spouses can be caregivers, the majority of caregivers for older adults are not spouses, but are younger family members living as part of the household. In these circumstances, older adults need sources of income, and they need younger, non-spouse, family members, either to provide transfers (when other sources of income are not available) and/or live in their households as caregivers. Table 9.1, based on the 10/66 group's data, shows that many older adults do not have any source of income and do not have younger family members in their

Table 9.1   *Social protection for people over 65 years in Latin America, India, and China*

Country	Source of Income			Vulnerable Living Arrangements		Total %
	Pension %	Family Transfers %	Paid Work %	Living Alone %	Living with Spouse Only %	
Cuba	82.1	8.9	10.0	8.9	27.3	36.2
Dominican Rep.	30.4	29.0	8.2	12.6	21.8	34.4
Venezuela	57.5	5.2	5.2	3.1	16.5	19.6
Peru (Urban)	65.7	4.9	0.9	3.3	16.8	21.1
Peru (Rural)	64.7	0.7	1.4	8.0	21.6	29.6
Mexico (Urban)	72.7	11.2	7.3	10.6	15.1	25.7
Mexico (Rural)	25.4	18.8	12.4	11.2	15.6	26.8
China (Urban)	90.5	4.7	0.0	4.7	49.2	53.9
China (Rural)	3.8	36.4	0.6	4.9	21.9	26.8
India (Urban)	11.6	37.8	2.4	4.4	15.9	20.3
India (Rural)	34.6	46.8	15.8	12.0	18.7	30.7

Source: The table is an abbreviated version of Table II in Prince et al. (2008), op. cit.

households able to act as caregivers. Family transfers are not always sufficient to fill the gap.[3]

Consider the extent of social protection in Table 9.1 for older adults in China. In rural areas, only 40.8 percent have some source of income, which means that most (59.2 percent) of the rural Chinese older adults have no source of income. As many as 26.8 percent live alone or with a spouse and therefore have vulnerable living arrangements, where there are no family caregivers available in the households. Even in the urban areas, where the vast majority (95.2 percent) have some source of income (pension), the majority (53.9 percent) of older adults in China live without any family members and so are classed as having vulnerable living arrangements. The UN conventions have certainly not guaranteed the social protection of older adults in China. A separate convention for the human rights of older adults is required.

As for what a new convention could contain, there already is a basic plan laid out in an earlier UN world assembly called the 2002 Madrid International Plan of Action on Ageing (MIPA) adopted by 159 nations.[4] This comprehensively covers dementia and how to intervene. Paragraph 86(c) covers people with dementia:

> Provide programmes to help persons with Alzheimer's disease and mental illness due to other sources of dementia to be able to live at home for as long as possible and to respond to their health needs.

In addition, paragraph 86(d) refers to providing support for caregivers of those with dementia:

> Develop programmes to support self-help and provide respite care for patients, families and other carers.

It also addresses dementia as a disability in paragraph 89:

> The ageing of persons with cognitive disabilities is a factor that should be considered in planning and decision-making processes.

And specifically it addresses how to deal with dementia disability in paragraph 90(c):

> Provide physical and mental rehabilitation services for older persons with disabilities.

This emphasis on mental rehabilitation as an intervention mirrors the UN 2006 Convention of the Rights of Persons with Disabilities that we covered earlier. Article 26(1) outlines the right of people with disability to attain maximum independence, with the assistance of comprehensive rehabilitation services. As has been pointed out: "We are used to thinking of rehabilitation in terms of physical rehabilitation following injury, but it is equally relevant for people with cognitive, rather than physical, rehabilitations. This includes people whose impairments result from long term degenerative diseases."[5] As an intervention, this is called "cognitive rehabilitation" (and we cover this in detail in the next section).

More generally, MIPA focuses on three priority areas:

- Older persons and development;
- Advancing health and well-being into old age; and
- Ensuring enabling and supportive environments.

It is so comprehensive that some countries at the UN have argued that a new convention for older adults is not necessary. However, Table 9.1 informs us otherwise. Even with two conventions and MIPA, many older adults do not have social protection. Globally, 68 percent of the world's population receive a pension. However, it is only 26 per cent in Central and Southern Asia and 23 percent in SSA.[6] How can people with dementia, who cannot work in paid employment and do not receive family financial support, expect to survive without a pension?

The essential difference between MIPA and a proposed new convention for older adults, which is now a work in progress,[7] is that the proposed new convention would be legally binding. This would ensure that not only will laws be initiated that protect the specific rights of older persons (like Australia's 2008 Fair Works Act), there would also be mechanisms in place to ensure that any initiated laws will be implemented and enforced. For example, a designated budget to finance carrying out the legislation would be allocated.

COGNITIVE REHABILITATION

Researchers working on evaluations of CR have from the outset accepted the premise that dementia is a disability. From this perspective, what is highlighted is the distinction between any disease's pathological changes, and the resulting limitations on engaging in activity and restrictions in social participation that come from that disease. Activity limitation and participation restriction can be termed functional disability. Functional disability need not be solely determined by the severity of the disease as it is also determined by a range of personal, social, and environmental influences. By changing these influences, an intervention that will be called rehabilitation, functional disability can be reduced even though the disease itself may not be affected. Rehabilitation is usually associated with non-progressive physical diseases and injuries. But, when it is involved with cognitive impairment involved with neurodegenerative diseases, such as dementia that can be progressive, the attempt to change the functional disability can be called CR.[8]

The particular functional disability that is changed is very individualized. Each client, which consists of the person with dementia and the main caregiver (called a "dyad"), sets a specific goal, related to self-care or a particular participation activity. The specific goal that is to be set is negotiated collaboratively between the client (the dyad) and an occupational therapist. The goal is person centered and is a compromise between what the client would most like to do, and what is feasible, given the symptoms of the person with dementia, the characteristics of the caregiver, and the home environment. Once the goal has been set, the intervention is tailored to achieving the goal. Hence, the main CR intervention is called the Tailored Activity Program (TAP) and we will be focusing exclusively on this version.[9]

The strength of this approach is that the client pair gets to decide what is the functional disability that is to be changed (that is, consumer sovereignty is involved). The weakness of this approach from a public policy and CBA perspective is that, because it is so individual specific, one does not have a homogeneous intervention to compare across individuals. How does one compare restoring one person's ability to go out alone with another person's restored ability to make a cup of tea? How can one use a common valuation method for such disparate outcomes?

The main solution devised by the CR evaluation literature related to TAP is to capture the functional disability outcome that was changed by the intervention in terms of the time that is freed up for the caregiver. There were two types of caregiving time that were saved: hours actually "doing things" for the dementia patient (such as managing self-care) and hours spent feeling that one needs to be there "on duty" for the dementia patient (by oversight demands involving guidance and assuring safety).

The causation strategy employed was to use a clinical control trial (as with the EAFC evaluation in the last chapter) with the treatment group receiving TAP and the control group receiving no TAP (but were put on a TAP waiting list). The estimated statistical outcome was the difference in caregiver time between the two groups.

ESTIMATING THE THREE STEPS FOR THE BENEFITS OF THE TAILORED ACTIVITY PROGRAM

We again refer to the benefits formula:

$$B = [\textit{Valuation}] \text{ of } [\textit{Change in Quantity}] \text{ from } [\textit{Change in Dementia}]$$
$$\text{from an intervention}$$

Steps 1 and 2

For the TAP intervention, it is not the dementia symptoms that are necessarily changed by the intervention (memory may not be restored). Instead, it is the disruptive behavior of dementia (agitation, aggressiveness, or resistance to care) that is changed. This disruptive behavior change, which is individual specific, can be standardized by quantifying the effect of this change in behavior according to the caregiver's time that is freed up by the intervention. As a result, the time freed up is the combination of steps 1 and 2 in the benefits formula from the TAP intervention and becomes comparable across clients.

For the TAP intervention, there were eight sessions of occupational therapy over a four-month period (120 days). It was implemented in three phases. Phase 1 involved the assessment by the interventionist of the client's circumstances (covering the dementia patient's abilities, deficits, habits and interests, and the caregiver activities and home environment). Phase 2 was based on the assessment results and these led to activity prescriptions. Three targeted activities were developed according to the patient's capabilities. Practice sessions were arranged for each of the targeted activities with the clients and the interventionist. In subsequent home visits, activity prescriptions were reviewed and modified. In phase 3, as caregivers mastered the activities, interventionists helped generalize the techniques to other care challenges (like resistance to bathing or dressing) and helped simplify the activities (in case the patient's abilities declined). These were the time savings for the caregivers:

- Time "doing things": 3.3 hours a day for 120 days equals 396 hours.
- Time "on duty": 6.9 hours a day for 120 days equals 828 hours.

Step 3

In the initial TAP evaluation, the method used to value the benefits was the same as was used for the education and Medicare eligibility CBAs, and that method was to estimate caregiver cost savings. In the TAP evaluation, if the caregiver had paid someone else to do the caregiving, as a conservative estimate, time saved was valued at the federal minimum wage of $7.25 per hour.[10] Using this valuation, the "doing things" benefits was estimated to be $2,872 and the "on duty" benefits were $6,003. The total benefits were therefore $8,875 over the course of the intervention.

ESTIMATING THE COSTS OF TAP

The costs covered the caregiver's time being trained, and the interventionist expenses in giving the training for the 120-day (four-month)
program. The cost categories and their estimates were:

- Training and supervision of interventionists: $10.08.
- Caregiver time in intervention: $55.35.
- Assessment materials: $76.73.
- Intervention supplies: $59.82.
- Interventionist time in sessions, preparation and documentation:
  $302.48.
- Interventionist travel time to and from participant's home: $330.48.
- Interventionist travel mileage cost to and from participant's home:
  $106.21.

The total TAP per-person cost was $942.

THE CBA OF THE TAILORED ACTIVITY
PROGRAM

With the benefits of $8,875, and the costs of $942, the net-benefits per
person were highly positive at $7,933 with a cost-benefit ratio of 9.42.
If the time savings were valued at the regional home health aide hourly
rate of $10.14 (which was used to value the caregiver's training time in
the cost part of the evaluation), the result would have been even more
socially worthwhile with net-benefits of $11,469 and a benefit-cost ratio
of 13.18.

In a recent re-evaluation of the TAP, an alternative monetary valuation of the time savings was considered.[11] The method involved asking
caregivers the amount that they were willing to pay to receive nursing
home services. For "on duty" time the valuation was $4.58 per hour,
which was less than the federal minimum wage of $7.25 per hour; but
the "doing things" time (which requires more effort from the caregiver)
was valued higher at $9.57 per hour. Multiplying these time values by the
828 hours saved "on duty" and the 396 hours saved "doing things," the
resulting "on duty" benefits were $3,792, and the "doing things" benefits
were $3,790. The total benefits of TAP were now estimated to be $7,582.
This was slightly lower than the $8,875 benefits figure used in the initial
valuation. However, the net-benefits were still positive at $6,640 with

a benefit-cost ratio of 8.05. The re-evaluation confirmed that the TAP intervention was indeed highly socially worthwhile, even using a different method for evaluating the benefits.

RELEVANCE OF THE TAP EVALUATION FOR LMICS

Although there are no existing CBAs of TAP interventions in LMICs, extensive groundwork has already been laid for adapting the TAP to LMICs. Brazil has its own version (TAP-BR) which ensures that the behavioral symptoms instrument that was used was relevant in Brazil's settings.[12] Also, the "Caregiver's Guide to Dementia," which is an important part of TAP, was modified to reflect the Brazilian context. This Guide provides examples of strategies for addressing behavioral symptoms including how to use the activities to mitigate them.

The causal effectiveness of TAP was established by a randomized clinical trial. The main outcome measure was the Brazilian version of the QoL scale, for both the person with dementia and the caregiver. For the caregiver, the QoL at the 120-day follow-up period increased significantly from baseline. For the person with dementia, the result depended on which person's QoL measure one was relying on. According to the caregiver's assessment of the QoL of the person with dementia, the QoL increased. However, from the perspective of the person with dementia's self-assessment of the QoL, no improvement took place. Since TAP interventions mainly (but not exclusively) focus on the caregiver perspective, the Brazilian TAP can be judged an overall effective intervention. All that is needed to convert the Brazilian TAP effectiveness outcome into a CBA evaluation is to put a monetary valuation on the QoL effects, as was done with the new interventions, and provide estimates of the costs of TAP, along the lines of the US TAP CBAs.

CHAPTER SUMMARY AND CONCLUSIONS

Protecting human rights, preventing elder abuse, and caring for older adults with dementia are all interlinked. An intervention (such as a proposed new UN convention) that promotes human rights is an intervention for persons with dementia, their caregivers, and an intervention for elder abuse. For example:

- If those with dementia have their human rights protected, they are more likely to be provided with an intervention like HAs and CL that decreases symptoms. With a decrease in symptoms, they are less vulnerable to elder abuse.
- If caregivers have their human rights protected, they are more likely to be provided with the financial means to care for those with dementia, and receive CR support as an intervention. CR can both decrease dementia symptoms for the patient and reduce the consequences of dementia symptoms for the caregiver. With less stress for the caregiver, elder abuse will be reduced.

CR is already an intervention specified as a human right under the 2006 UN Convention on the Rights of Persons with Disabilities. What is missing is the enforcement of this human right, as social protection for the elderly has been shown to be lacking. A new human rights convention for older adults would help to remedy this deficiency, and could include special provision for CR. An important contribution of this chapter was to apply our three-step procedure for estimating benefits, to confirm that the main example of CR (the TAP) was not only a human right, but also socially worthwhile.

Note that the Compassionate Allowance Initiative (CAI) in the USA helps expedite the process for applying for Social Security Disability Insurance (for those who worked long enough and paid social security taxes) and Supplemental Security Income (for those aged 65 or older, blind or disabled). The CAI was designed to aid those with obvious disabilities and this explicitly mentions as a disability those with the various categories of dementia. Including CAI as a provision in a proposed new human rights convention for older adults would also facilitate social protection for all persons with dementia. It is not enough that social protection programs exist; people with dementia need to have access to those programs.

One reason why CR is an important final intervention for this book to consider is that it complements the new interventions for dementia that were presented in earlier chapters. Central to the evaluation of the new interventions was the outcome that symptoms would decline, and in this way, activities of daily living would be re-established. With CR, the dementia symptoms need not be reduced, yet some of the daily living activities can be restored. Persons with dementia may now be able to walk round the block unaccompanied. This can take place when an occupational therapist has trained them how to use a cell phone to connect them with their caregiver, whenever help is needed for that person to return home safely.

The other main reason why CR is an important final intervention for this book to evaluate is that it provides, in practical terms, an application of the central reality of dementia, that directly, or indirectly, everyone is affected by dementia. People can develop dementia symptoms themselves and it is important that these symptoms be reduced by socially worthwhile interventions, as we have demonstrated. However, often just as important is the fact that those without dementia may end up being a caregiver for someone with dementia. CR adds the perspective that interventions need to be evaluated that also address the needs of caregivers. Looking after someone with dementia creates enormous stress for the caregiver. This stress may lead to elder abuse for the person with dementia, but it also extracts an enormous toll on the caregiver, as we now explain.

The spouses of persons with dementia have been called "invisible second patients."[13] This is because a population-based study found that such spouses are six times more likely to develop dementia than persons whose spouses have not experienced dementia. Stratified by gender, the exposure to dementia was much higher for men (11.9 times) than for women (3.7 times).[14] These results were obtained using many of the same controls that we used to establish causality with the new interventions we have presented, including education, age, gender, and the APOE e4 gene. The biological reason for the family caregiver results is that caregiving for persons with dementia creates stress, and stress damages the brain. Obviously, couples that have lived a long time together (it was on average 48.9 years in the study) have to radically change their lifestyles when one person develops dementia, and this inevitably creates stress.

CR, in the form of the TAP program in the USA, produced benefits around 9.4 times greater than the costs, and so has been found to be very socially worthwhile. The TAP program has already been adapted to the cultural circumstances of LMICs and found to be very effective. Given that dementia creates stress universally, there is every reason to think that CR will also become a socially worthwhile dementia intervention in LMICs, when it is subject to a full cost-benefit evaluation.

BOOK SUMMARY AND CONCLUSIONS

The presence of behavioral symptoms defines dementia and not brain pathology. The reality of this statement was confirmed by the 2020 Report of the Lancet Commission – hereafter referred to as "the 2020 Report."[15] This pointed out that most persons with normal cognition, who also have amyloid plaques and tau tangles in their brains, never develop the disease. Therefore, we began the book emphasizing that we do not have to wait for breakthroughs in medical science or pharmaceutical technologies to reduce dementia symptoms today.

The dementia literature has identified effective interventions that already exist. We mentioned as examples changing one's diet, sleep patterns, and exercise regimes. The purpose of this book is to add to the list of known interventions, five new interventions: years of education, Medicare eligibility, hearing aids, vision correction, and avoiding nursing homes. What makes these five interventions "new" is not that nobody knows about them – some of them (like education) have been extensively analysed in the literature, and are at least mentioned somewhere in the 2020 Report. What is new is that they all for the first time have been explicitly shown to be causally effective, and all now have been explicitly shown to be socially worthwhile.

Establishing the effectiveness of any given intervention is a challenge, but essential. One main part of the book was devoted to explaining, in minimally technical terms, some of the main difficulties and solutions to establishing causality for dementia interventions. Hence, how causality was established was a main part of the analysis for each of the evaluations of the five new interventions presented. In the 2020 Report, the importance of establishing causality was referred to a number of times (for example, "association does not prove causality").[16] But the establishment of causality was not treated as a prerequisite for any of the risk factors that they were recommending as interventions. Instead, they stated that "we have *assumed* [my emphasis] a causal relationship between risk factors and dementia" and "that *at least some* [my emphasis] of the risk factors estimated here do have a causal relationship."[17] It is not the case that one can ever prove causality in economics and medicine beyond a shadow of a doubt (one can always come up with some confounding evidence). But researchers have the responsibility to state their case why causality is strongly indicated when they present their estimates of the effectiveness of any intervention, which is what we tried to do. Note that four of the 2020 Report's "risk factors" (age, family history, gender, and APOE e4) were used as controls to establish effectiveness for the five new interventions we evaluated.

Nevertheless, establishing effectiveness is not a sufficient achievement in order to undertake public policy decisions to approve any particular dementia intervention. An effective intervention has to pass an economic evaluation checking that it is socially worthwhile. For this purpose, CBA must be used. Output effects are to be valued in monetary terms to be designated as "benefits," in order to be compared to the costs, which are usually already measured in monetary terms. The amount of the benefits generated by any intervention must be compared to the monetary costs of the intervention to see if they are larger. Only if the estimated benefits exceed the costs can an intervention be judged to be socially worthwhile and thereby justify funding. Therefore, the other main part of the book was to explain some basic CBA principles in order to apply them to undertake each of the economic evaluations of the new interventions.

CBA has been grossly underutilized in the health care field in general, and in the area of dementia in particular. The standard justification for not using CBA is that it is often difficult to estimate benefits.[18] But, being "difficult" does not mean impossible to achieve. There are dozens of different ways to put a value on an output to produce an estimate of benefits.[19] For each of the five interventions in this book we used a slightly different method. The two general CBA principles we used for our methods was that of cost savings and putting a price on a QALY.

For the education evaluation, we used the cost savings in caregiving, from people whose dementia symptoms are reduced and are thereby more able to move to independent living. The Medicare eligibility evaluation used a similar method as for education, except that it allowed for the fact that reducing dementia symptoms also increases the person's QoL, This in turn enables the person whose symptoms have been reduced to be more willing to seek independent living, making the cost savings for caregivers even larger. For the hearing aids, vision correction, and nursing home avoidance evaluations we used the price of a QALY and applied it to a QALY and its parts. We worked with just the QoL part of a QALY (for the HA intervention); worked with just the LY part of a QALY (for the VC intervention); and finally worked with both LY and QoL parts of a QALY (for the NH avoidance intervention).

The most general CBA valuation principle is to use Willingness to Pay (WTP). The logic is that if someone pays the market price for something, such as a car for $50,000, the car must be valued at least this amount, or else the person would not have bought it (if they were rational and well informed). We did not use WTP for any of our five new interventions for the simple reason that persons with dementia cannot be expected to earn income, and thus income was not a variable in our NACC data set. Without an income, a person does not have the ability to pay for anything. Nonetheless, caregivers do have incomes, or have to forego incomes to care for someone. Therefore, when we presented a CBA of an existing intervention for CR in this chapter, we did give an application of WTP, in terms of the hours that were saved by CR being effective, and applied various wage rates to those saved hours.

For each of the five new interventions, we applied a three-step procedure for estimating the benefits. First, the intervention must lower dementia symptoms. Second, the reduction in symptoms from the intervention must produce an output change that society cares about. And third, a price/value must be attached to that output change. This three-step procedure can be applied to any dementia intervention, and not just the five new interventions with which we have been mainly concerned. Thus, we used this three-step procedure to carry out the CBAs in the last chapter on elder abuse, and in this chapter on human rights, that were first evaluated in the dementia literature.

The 2020 Report did analyse the effectiveness of the evidence for some interventions for dementia. But, what was missing was the reporting of the monetary costs and benefits of these interventions. Without mentioning costs and benefits, they made three main recommendations:[20]

- Provide holistic post-diagnostic care.
- Manage neuropsychiatric symptoms.
- Care for family carers.

The 2020 Report did state that care for family carers was cost-effective. However, cost-effectiveness analysis does not get the job done, in regards to deciding whether an intervention is socially worthwhile or not, and in determining expenditure priorities. An intervention can be very cost-effective, yet not be worthwhile (benefits are less than costs); and an intervention can be not cost-effective, yet still be worthwhile (benefits exceed costs). In this case, the cost-ineffective intervention should be given priority over the cost-efficient intervention. Consequently, there is little valid basis for the 2020 Report conclusion that: "Although we have more to learn about effectiveness, avoiding or delaying even a proportion of potentially modifiable dementias should be a national priority for all."[21]

The importance of using CBA to help decide dementia intervention priorities, for medical or non-medical interventions, cannot be overstated. Consider this scenario. The *World Alzheimer Report 2018* states that: "anyone who knows anything about the disease knows that there is not going to be a magic pill." They add: "It's likely, to be a multiple set of treatments and drugs."[22] However, let us assume, for sake of argument, that a magic dementia pill has been invented and this cures and prevents dementia entirely (unlike Aduhelm). This does not automatically guarantee that this magic dementia pill should be a national expenditure priority. Does it not matter how much it costs? Say it costs $1,000 a day for this magic dementia pill, which becomes a cost of $365,000 per year. Does it not matter how large are the benefits? If the benefits were valued at less than $365,000, the magic dementia pill would not be judged socially worthwhile and should not be approved.

In this book, we have used $500,000 to value a year of life with the highest QoL. On this basis, the hypothetical magic dementia pill would have been judged worthwhile. Nonetheless, even in this case, it may not be a national priority. The magic dementia pill's benefit-cost ratio of 1.37 would place it well behind in priority all the new interventions we have analysed. The benefit-cost ratios were:[23]

- Nearly 3.93 for the Check & Connect school dropout prevention program;
- It was 1.43 for Medicare eligibility (even without including any other health care benefits than reducing dementia symptoms);
- It was 29.23 for hearing aids;
- It was 18.63 for vision correction; and
- It was effectively infinite for avoiding living in nursing homes (there were benefits, but no costs).

Thus, the fundamental problem with the 2020 Report is that it tries to provide recommendations, and talk about national dementia expenditure priorities, without any detailed reference to the costs and benefits of any of their reported interventions.

The five new dementia intervention CBAs that we carried out relied on measuring dementia by using the University of Washington's Clinical Dementia Rating Scale, known as the *CDR® Dementia Staging Instrument*. To provide a brief summary of this instrument, and to illustrate its widespread usefulness, we will look at each of the six domains and see how they would be relevant measures for explaining why family caretakers of persons with dementia are susceptible to getting dementia themselves due to the stress involved.

Say a family caretaker has spent the last hour subject to aggressive behavior, due to a delirium episode by the person with dementia. There should not be any surprise if the family caretakers:

- Forgot that they were supposed to call a friend about a lunch appointment.
- Thought they were arguing in the bedroom, but instead realized they were located in the kitchen.
- Had great difficulty deciding whether today was the day that it was necessary for the person with dementia to be transferred to a nursing home.
- Were not able to go out of the house to attend a community school board meeting.
- Were not able to practice playing the piano (a hobby).
- Did not have time to look after their appearance (personal care).

Dementia was defined as not being able to carry out the activities of daily living. Why would many of the ADLs of family members looking after persons with dementia not be interrupted?

The latest research tells us that the brain that we are born with is not a fixed entity. There is a large amount of brain plasticity, and this applies to people of all ages, even older adults with dementia.[24] Brain cells can be made to increase in number and interactions between brain cells (synapses) can be reconnected. The fact that age-specific dementia rates have fallen shows that existing interventions must have existed,[25] even though they may not be medical or pharmacological. This book adds five new ones. Investing in these interventions reduces elder abuse and promotes older adults' human rights. Our contribution is to show that these interventions are also socially worthwhile. Given that two-thirds of persons with dementia live in LMICs, these five new interventions should be given even higher priority in these countries than in the USA.

NOTES

1. http://www.claiminghumanrights.org/udhr_article_25.htm (accessed December 2021).
2. https://www.un.org/development/desa/disabilities/convention-on-the-rights -of-persons-with-disabilities/convention-on-the-rights-of-persons-with -disabilities-2.html (accessed December 2021).
3. Prince, M., Acosta, D., Albanese, E., Arizaga, R., Ferri, C.P., Guerra, M., et al. (2008), "Ageing and Dementia in Low and Middle Income Countries – Using Research to Engage with Public and Policy Makers", *International Review of Psychiatry*, 20, 332–343.
4. Second World Assembly on Ageing (2002), *Political Declaration and Madrid International Plan of Action on Ageing*, New York: United Nations.
5. Clare, L. (2017), "Rehabilitation for People Living with Dementia: A Practical Framework for Positive Support", *PLoS Medicine*, 14, e1002245.
6. United Nations (2018), *Promoting Inclusion through Social Protection: Report on the World Situation*, Department of Economic and Social Affairs. Chapter IV.
7. The United Nations 11th General Assembly Open-ended Working Group for Strengthening the Protection of the Human Rights of Older Persons took place on April 29–May 1, 2021. This group is working on establishing a new UN convention for the human rights of older adults.
8. Clare, L., Bayer, A., Burns, A., Corbett, A., Jones, R., Knapp, M., et al. (2013), "Goal-Oriented Cognitive Rehabilitation in Early-Stage Dementia: Study Protocol for a Multi-Centre Single-Blind Randomized Controlled Trial (GREAT)", *Trials*, 14, 152.
9. Gitlin, L.N,, Hodgson, N., Jutkowitz, E., Pizzi, L., and Pharm, D. (2010), "The Cost Effectiveness of a Nonpharmacologic Intervention for Individuals with Dementia and Family Caregivers: The Tailored Activity Program", *American Journal of Geriatric Psychiatry*, 18, 510–519.
10. Note that it is because Gitlin et al. (2010), op. cit., as cited in note 9, put a monetary value on their outcome unit, which is time in hours, that their TAP economic evaluation constitutes a CBA, although they call it a CEA.
11. Jutkowitz, E., Scerpella, D., Pizzi, L.T., Marx, K., Samus, Q., Pierso, C.V., and Gitlin, L.N. (2019), "Dementia Family Caregiver's Willingness to Pay for an In-home Program to Reduce Behavioral Symptoms and Caregiver Stress", *Pharmacoeconomics*, 37, 563–572.
12. Novelli, M.P.C., Machado, S.C.B., Lima, G.B., Cantatore, L., Sena, B.P., Rodrigues, C.I.B., et al. (2018), "Effects of the Tailored Activity Program in Brazil (TAP-BR) for Persons with Dementia: A Randomized Pilot Trial", *Alzheimer Disease and Associated Disorders*, 32, 339–345.
13. Gupta, S. (2020), *Keep Sharp: Build a Better Brain at Any Age*, New York: Simon & Schuster, page 273.
14. Norton, M.C., Smith, K.R., Ostbye, T., Tschanz, J.T., Corcoran, C., Schwartz, S., et al. (2010), "Increased Risk of Dementia When Spouse Has Dementia? The Cache County Study", *Journal of the American Geriatrics Society*, 58, 895–900.

15. Livingston, G., Huntley, J., Sommerlad, A., Ames, D., Ballard, C., Banerjee, S., et al. (2020), "Dementia Prevention, Intervention, and Care: 2020 Report of the Lancet Commission", *The Lancet*, 396, 413–446.
16. Ibid., page 429.
17. Ibid., pages 428 and 429.
18. For example, "Although popular in other fields, CBA is not commonly used in health technology assessment due to difficulty of associating monetary values with health outcomes such as (increased) survival." See Cost-Benefit Analysis [online]. (2016). York Health Economics Commission, York. https://yhec.co.uk/glossary/cost-benefit-analysis/.
19. See, for example, any textbook on applied CBA, such as Brent, R.J. (2006), *Applied Cost-Benefit Analysis*, 2nd edition, Cheltenham, UK and Northampton, MA, USA: Edward Elgar; and Brent, R.J. (2014), *Cost-Benefit Analysis and Health Care Evaluations*, 2nd edition, Cheltenham, UK and Northampton, MA, USA: Edward Elgar. For a simple introduction, see Brent, R.J. (2017), *Advanced Introduction to Cost-Benefit Analysis*, Cheltenham, UK and Northampton, MA, USA: Edward Elgar.
20. Livingston, G. et al. (2020), op. cit., key message, page 414.
21. Ibid., page 429.
22. Alzheimer's Disease International (2018), *World Alzheimer Report 2018. The State of the Art of Dementia Research: New Frontiers*, ADI: London, page 7.
23. We use benefit-cost ratios to compare outcomes here because it is easier to compare results than using net-benefit amounts. To be worthwhile, a benefit-cost ratio must be greater than 1. In general, when benefits are greater than costs (net-benefits are positive) it follows that the benefit-cost ratios are greater than 1. However, when there is a budget constraint, the test is that one should choose the interventions with the highest benefit cost ratios, which is the implicit test used in this paragraph of the chapter. See also note 15 of Chapter 6.
24. Gupta, S. (2020), op. cit., page 32.
25. Satizabal, C.L., Beiser, A.S., Chouraki, V., Chêne, G., Dufouil, C., and Seshadri, S. (2016), "Incidence of Dementia over Three Decades in the Framingham Heart Study", *New England Journal of Medicine*, 374, 523–532.

Index